426411

D1477025

Comics Feeeever!!

Uncover the power of comics in art and design

Edited & Published by
viction:ary

Comics Feeeever!!

Uncover the power of comics
in art and design

First published and distributed by
viction workshop ltd

viction:ary

viction workshop ltd
Unit C, 7/F, Seabright Plaza,
9-23 Shell Street,
North Point, Hong Kong
Url: www.victionary.com
Email: we@victionary.com
 www.facebook.com/victionworkshop
 www.twitter.com/victionary_
 www.weibo.com/victionary

Edited and produced by viction:ary

Concepts & art direction by Victor Cheung
Book design by viction workshop ltd

ISBN 978-988-12228-9-3
Printed and bound in China

Comics Feeeever!!

Uncover the power of comics in art and design

Edited & Published by
viction:ary

Forewoooorrrd!!

by Butcher Billy

Someone once said that Joy Division or The Smiths were not meant to be listened by the popular kids at school. You probably must be asking yourself why a line like that opens the foreword of a book about comics.

Well, when I was a kid in the 80s I was heavily influenced by everything from Saturday morning cartoons on TV to the music coming from the radio. Ian Curtis and Morrissey were as iconic to me as Batman and Superman. And comic books, at least back then, were definitely not meant to be read by the popular kids at school.

So yes, I was the typical shy and dysfunctional kid that saw in superhero comics, video games, movies, music and art some great ways to break free and also understand myself. I agree with Alex DeLarge - it's funny how the colours of the real world only seem really real when you see them on a screen.

Since then I became fascinated in exploring the multiple layers that separate fiction and reality, and the ways that they're always clashing and influencing each other. Real people or imaginary characters, the incorruptible ideals of perfect superheroes or the human flaws and desires sometimes so desperately depicted in song lyrics. The balance is what makes life larger than it really is.

And who doesn't want to be larger than life?! Imagine that even after your death you're kept in the collective memory - and future generations will have a blurry image of you keeping only your cool features. Let's get real - turning yourself into a pop culture icon is a great way to become immortal.

In the same way I realised video-games are a metaphor to our life - things will get harder and harder as you get closer to what you want the most. You live, you learn. You fall, you learn. Try again? Get a life and press start to continue.

And every time things become unbearable and you need to take a break between one level and the other - turn on the TV, get a cinema ticket or put on your headphones and press play. Also, of course, you can always open a book exactly like the one you have in your hands right now - full of speech balloons containing life's greatest secrets. You just have to read closely.

Ann Van Hoey
Armin Morbach
Aslan Malik
Ben Frost
Benoit Lapray
Butcher Billy
Chris Panda
COMMONROOOM
D*Face
Fantasista Utamaro
Forma & Co
Jeff Hong
Jon Walters Creative
Jonathan Calugi
JumpFromPaper
Lazy Oaf
Manasseh Langtimm Associates
Marek Okon
Mark Drew
Markus Hofko
Martín Vitaliti
Mika Tsutai
Moio Associates
nOir Jewelry
Noto Fusai
Óscar Gutiérrez Gonzalez
Paperform
Philip Colbert
Rémi Noël
Rex Koo
Romance Was Born
Sandra Chevrier
Schemata Architects
Shun Sasaki
Sim Chang
Teodoru Badiu
The Creative Method
THEROOM creative Ltd.
Tomasz Płonka

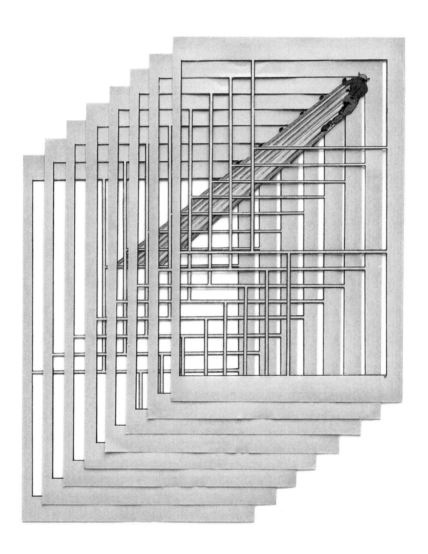

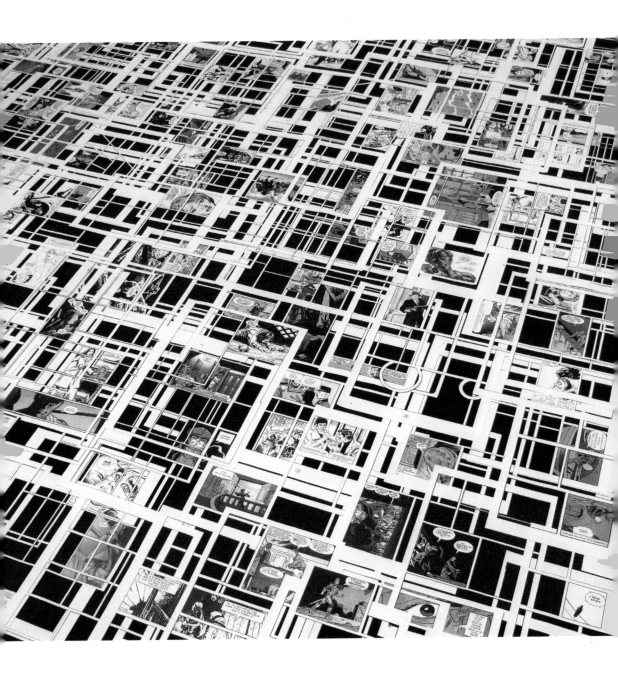

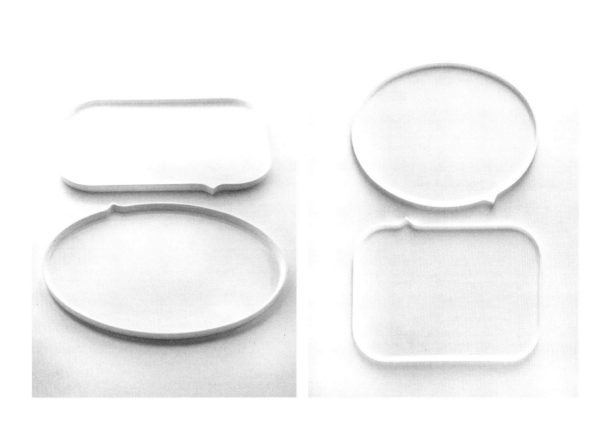

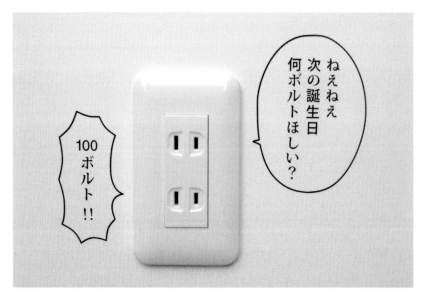

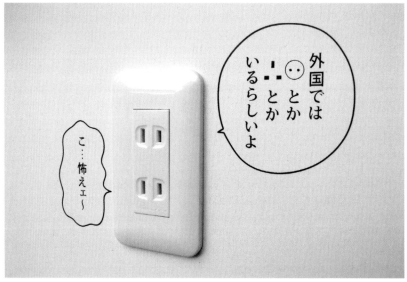

ちょっと
やだぁー
そんなに
じーっと
みないでよー

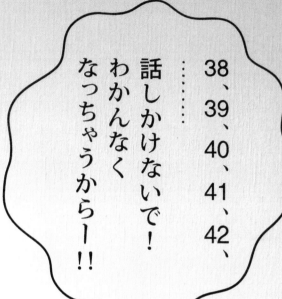

38、39、40、41、42、
……
話しかけないで！
わかんなく
なっちゃうからー!!

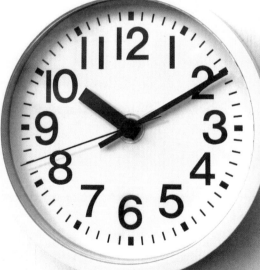

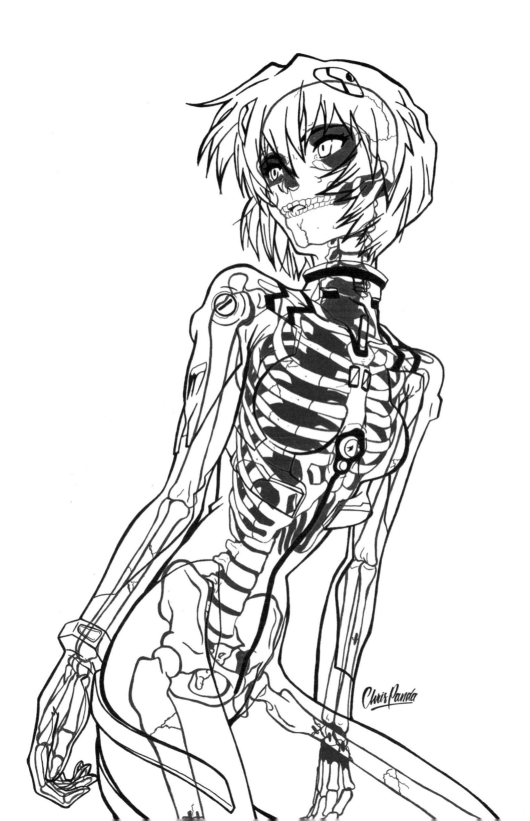

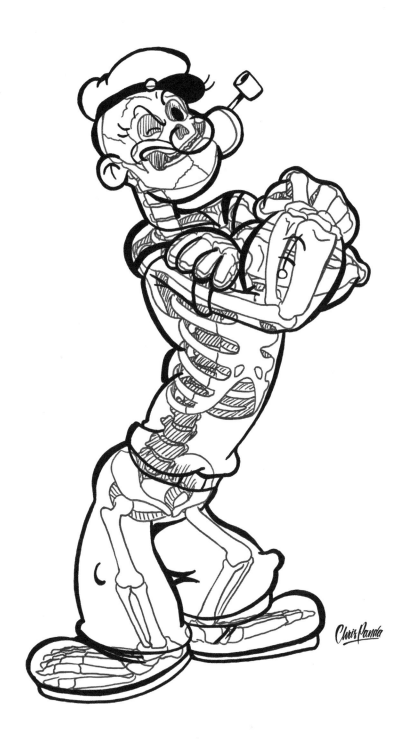

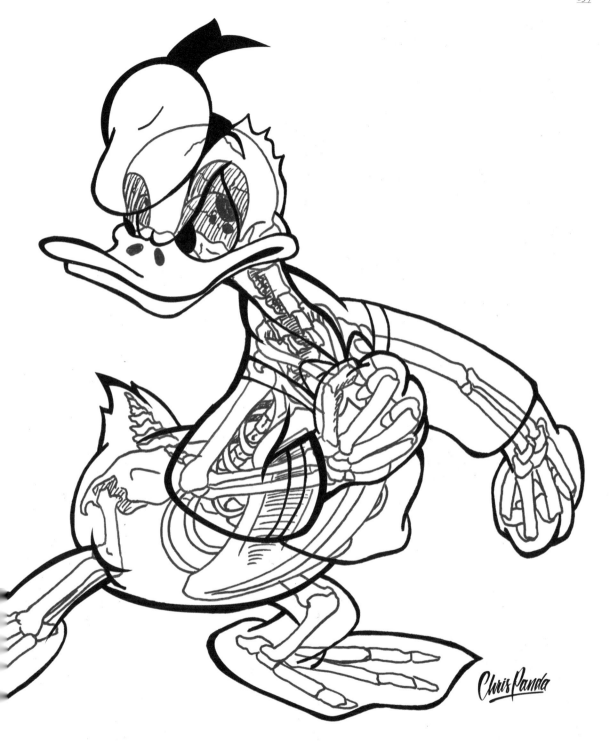

Chris Panda

Chris Panda

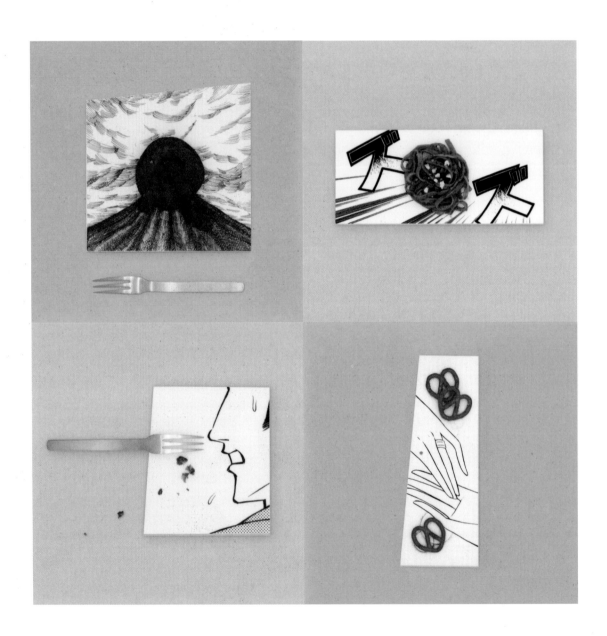

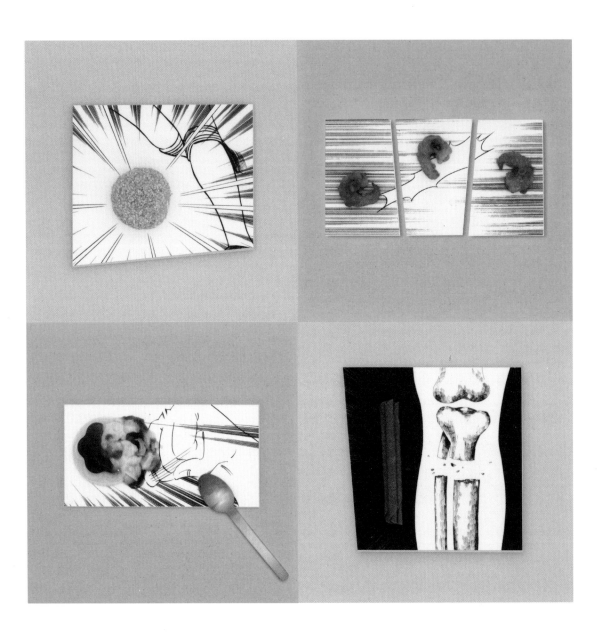

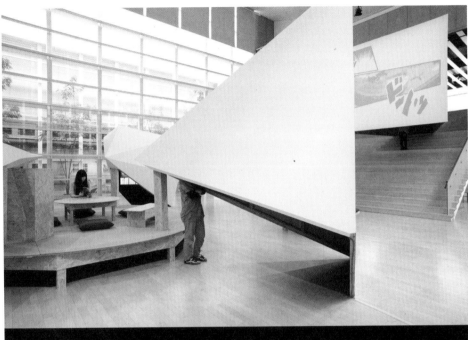

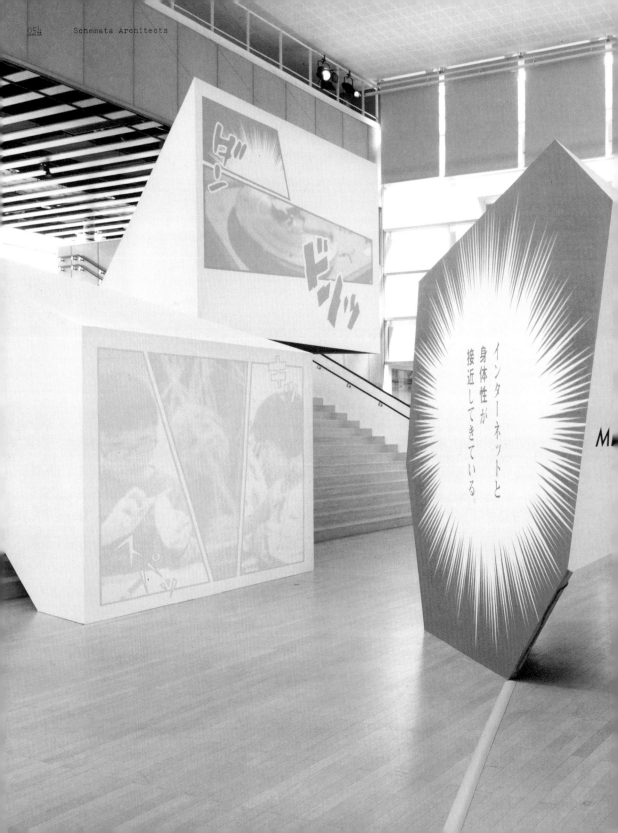

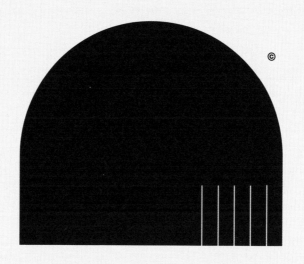

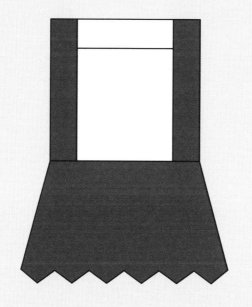

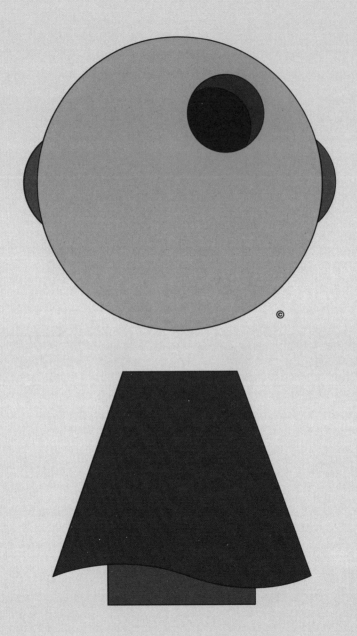

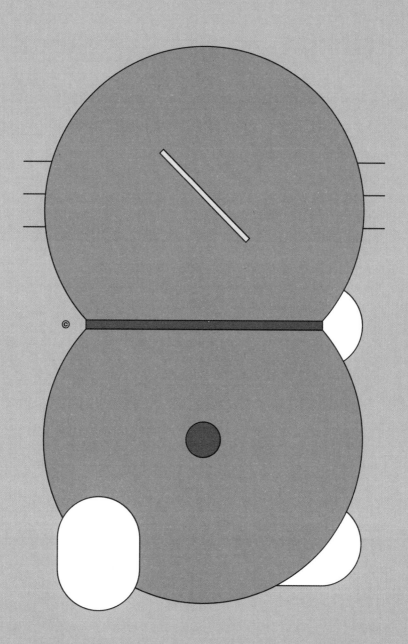

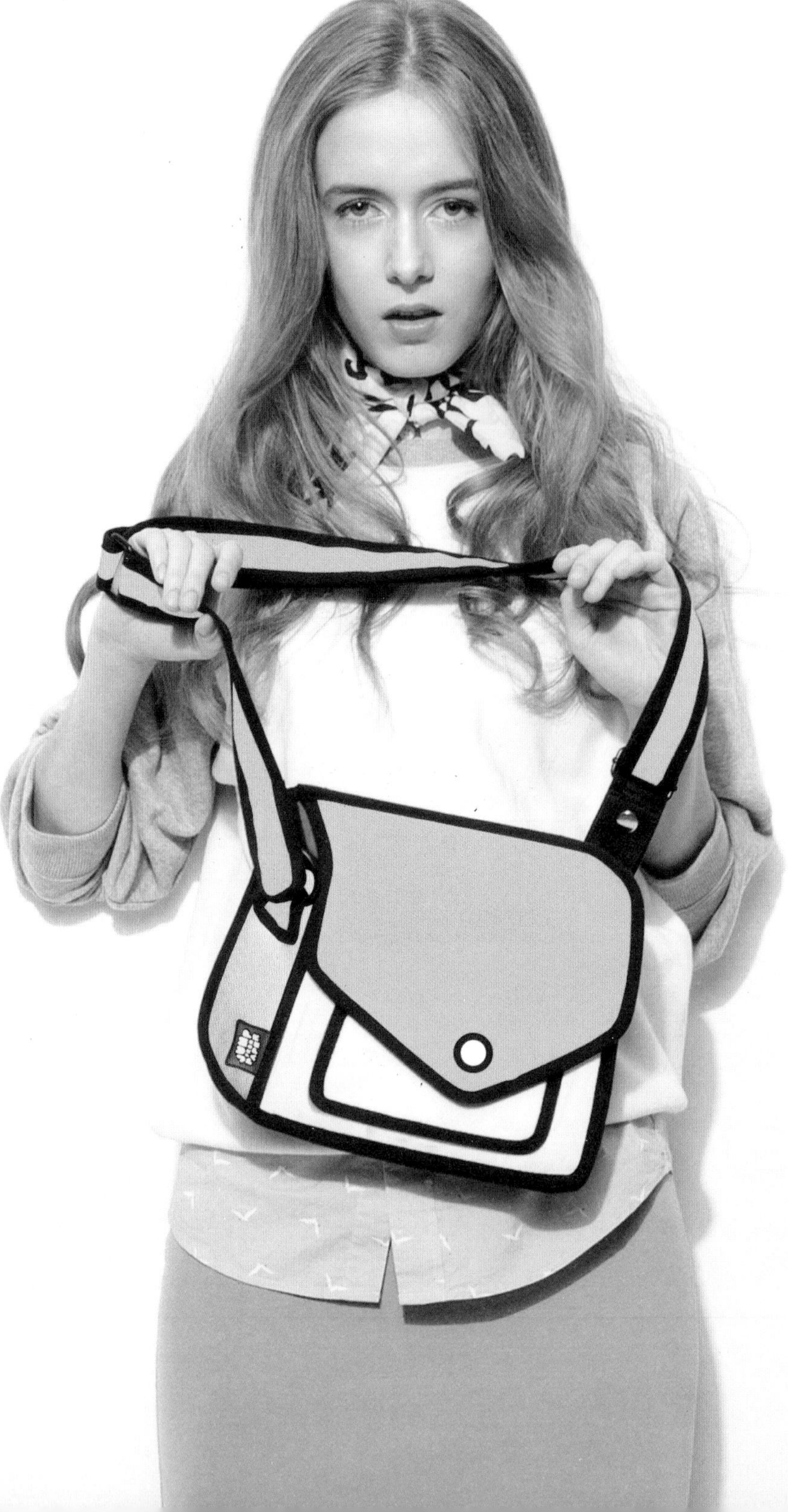

Fall / Winter 2013
FOOTWEAR & ACCESSORIES

ete !

Shop G26, Windsor House, Causeway Bay / Shop 108, Cityplaza, Taikoo Shing / Shop L113, THE ONE, Tsimshatsui / Shop B1-16, Langham Place, Mongkok / Shop G101, Plaza Hollywood, Diamond Hill
Shop G06, Mikiki, San Po Kong / Shop UC-15, APM, Kwun Tong / Shop 1086, Metro City Plaza II, Tseung Kwan O / Shop F47, POPCORN, Tseung Kwan O / Shop 139, Tsuen Wan Plaza, Tsuen Wan
Shop 2-01, Citistore, City Landmark II, Tsuen Wan / Shop 3282, Tuen Mun Town Plaza I, Tuen Mun / Shop 238C, Tai Po Mega Mall, Tai Po / Shop 312, Landmark North, Sheung Shui

www.ete.ithk.com   Instagram ete_hk

I.T IS INSPIRATION
www.ithk.com

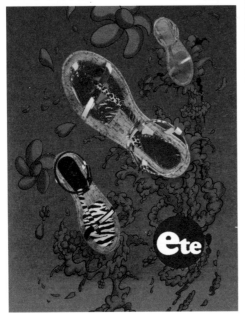

スピードは勝つ

NIKE ZOOM SPEED RACER 4

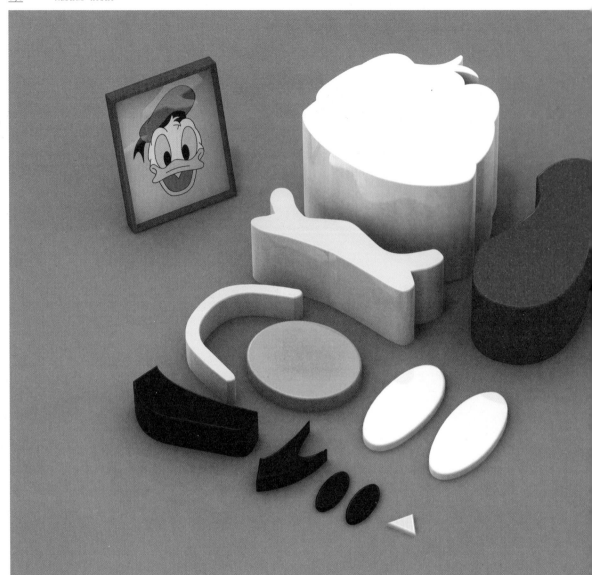

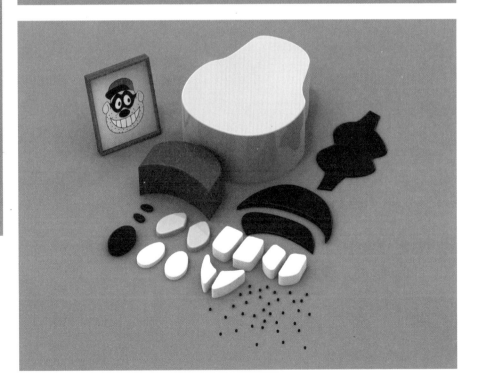

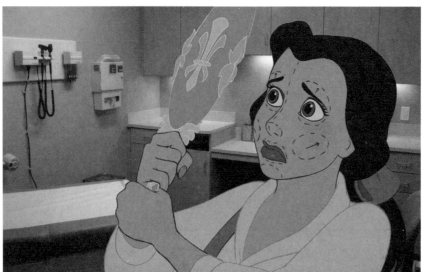

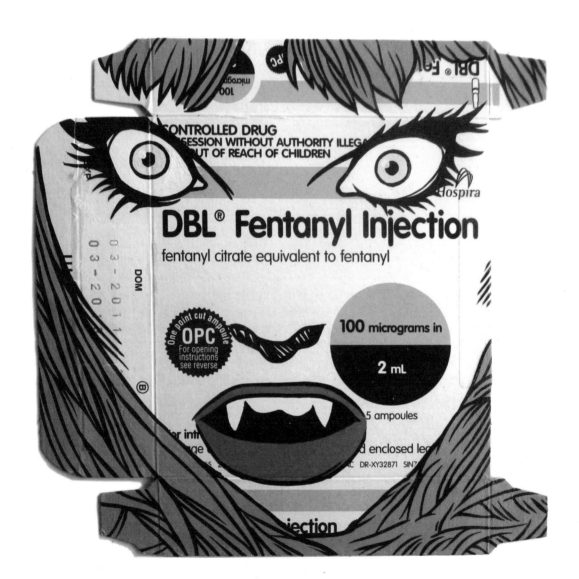

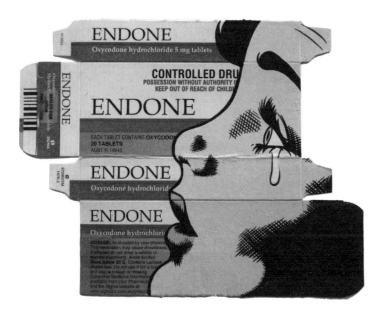

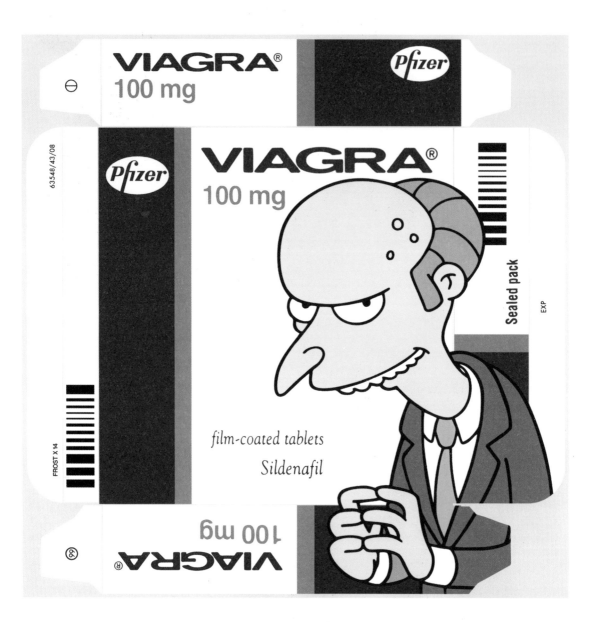

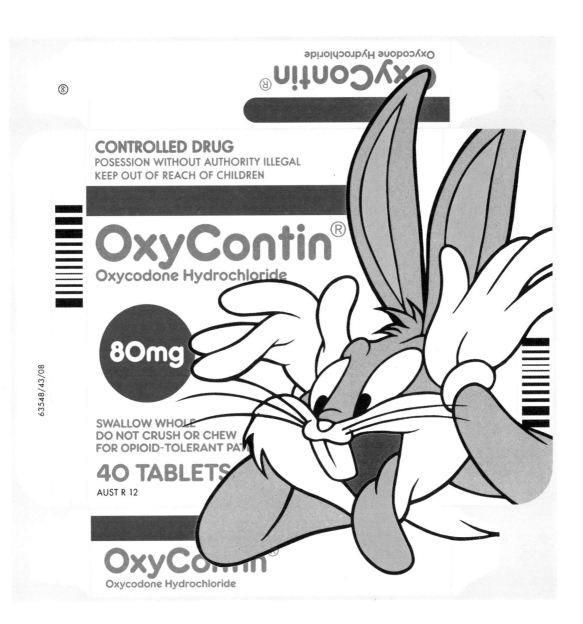

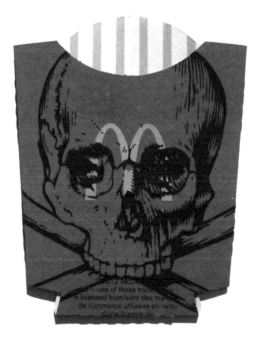

TOKYO BAR
www.Tokyobar-nyc.com

TOKYO BAR
www.tokyobar-nyc.com

TOKYO BAR

NEW JAPANESE COMFORT FOOD

277 Church St.

New York NY 10013

T 212·966·2787

F 212·219·2970

Open 11am~Midnight

www·tokyobar·nyc·com

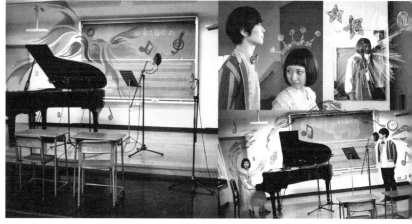

SUMMER 2012/2013

Romance Was Born

presents Berserkergang

Summer 2012/2013

SUMMER 2012/2013

CREATIVE DIRECTOR - MARK VASSALLO
PRODUCER - RACHEL TUFFERY @ PRONTO PRODUCTIONS
STYLIST - CATERINA SCARDINO @ COMPANY 1
MUSIC DIRECTOR - JONNY SEYMOUR
MAKE UP - NATASHA SEVERINO @ COMPANY 1 FOR MAC
HAIR - ALAN WHITE @ THE NAMES AGENCY FOR GHD
JEWELLERY AND BAGS - BVLGARI
SHOES - SIREN SHOES
NAILS BY NAIL ROCK FOR ASOS
PAPER ENGINEERING - BENJA HARNEY
GRAPHICS - BIRDY INGLIS AND HADEE
COLLECTION TEXT - TESS HEWITT
PR & SPONSORSHIP - LITTLE HERO
PRESS CONTACT - RWB@LITTLEHERO.COM.AU
SALES CONTACT - SALES@ROMANCEWASBORN.COM

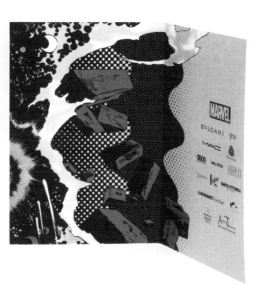

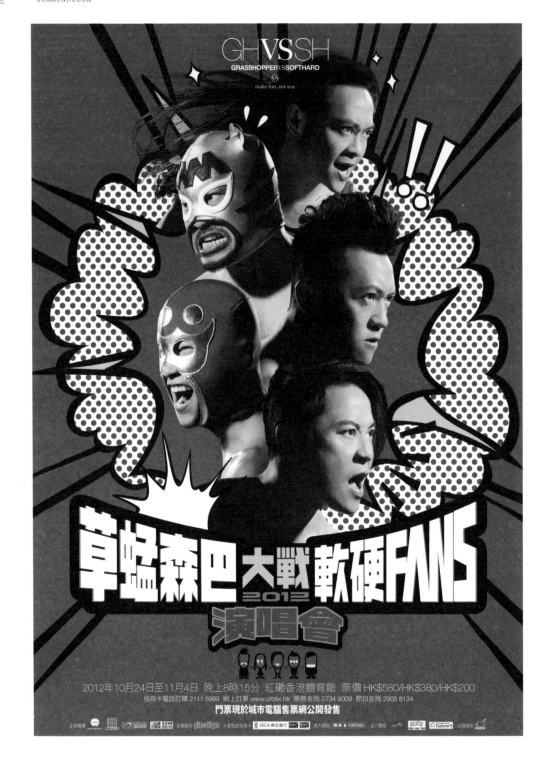

3OMETHING SCARY
林海峰 玩得開心啲

林海峰 玩得開心啲
有獎遊戲。
(請找出四處不同地方)

玩得開心啲。我好驚兩首新歌玩出四處不同版本
玩埋 YOYO／王菀之／ANGELITA／KETCHUP

林狗末日嬉戲。EP即日降臨

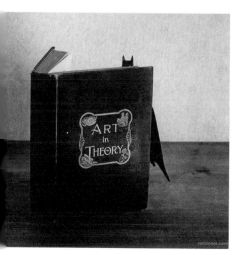

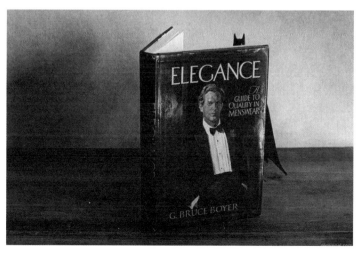

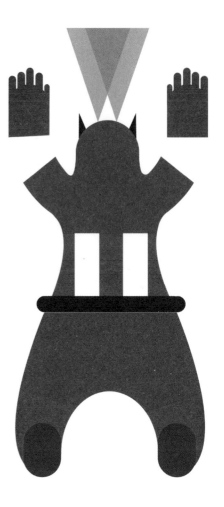

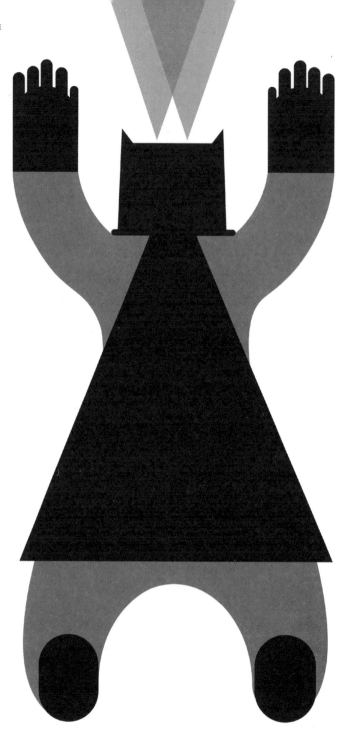

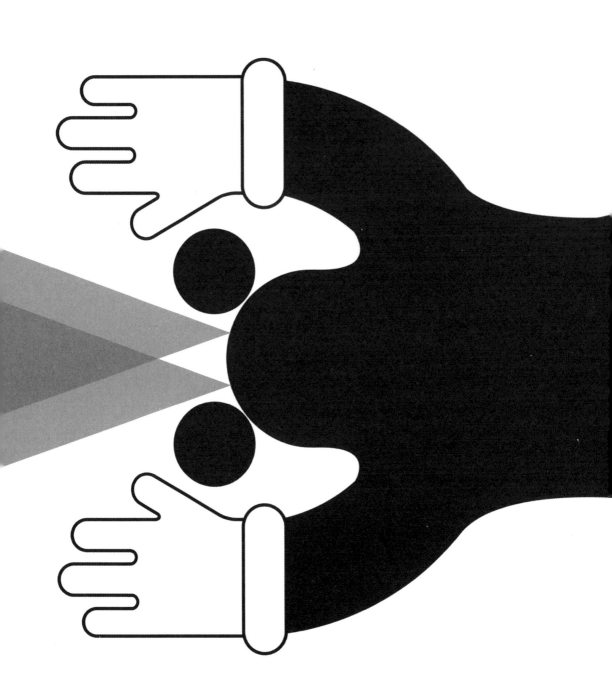

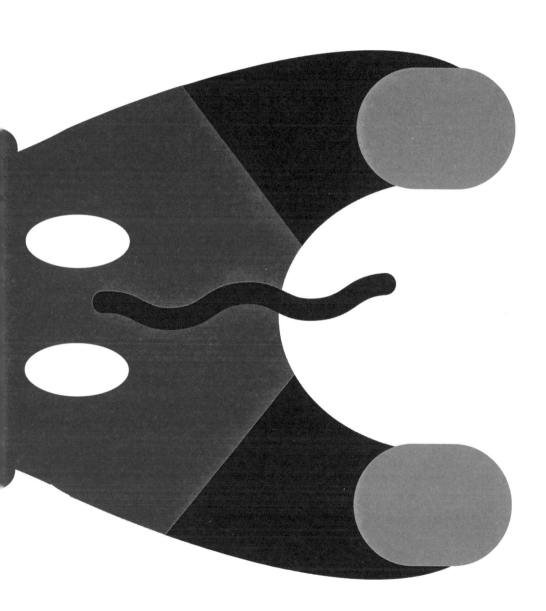

That's not all Folks!

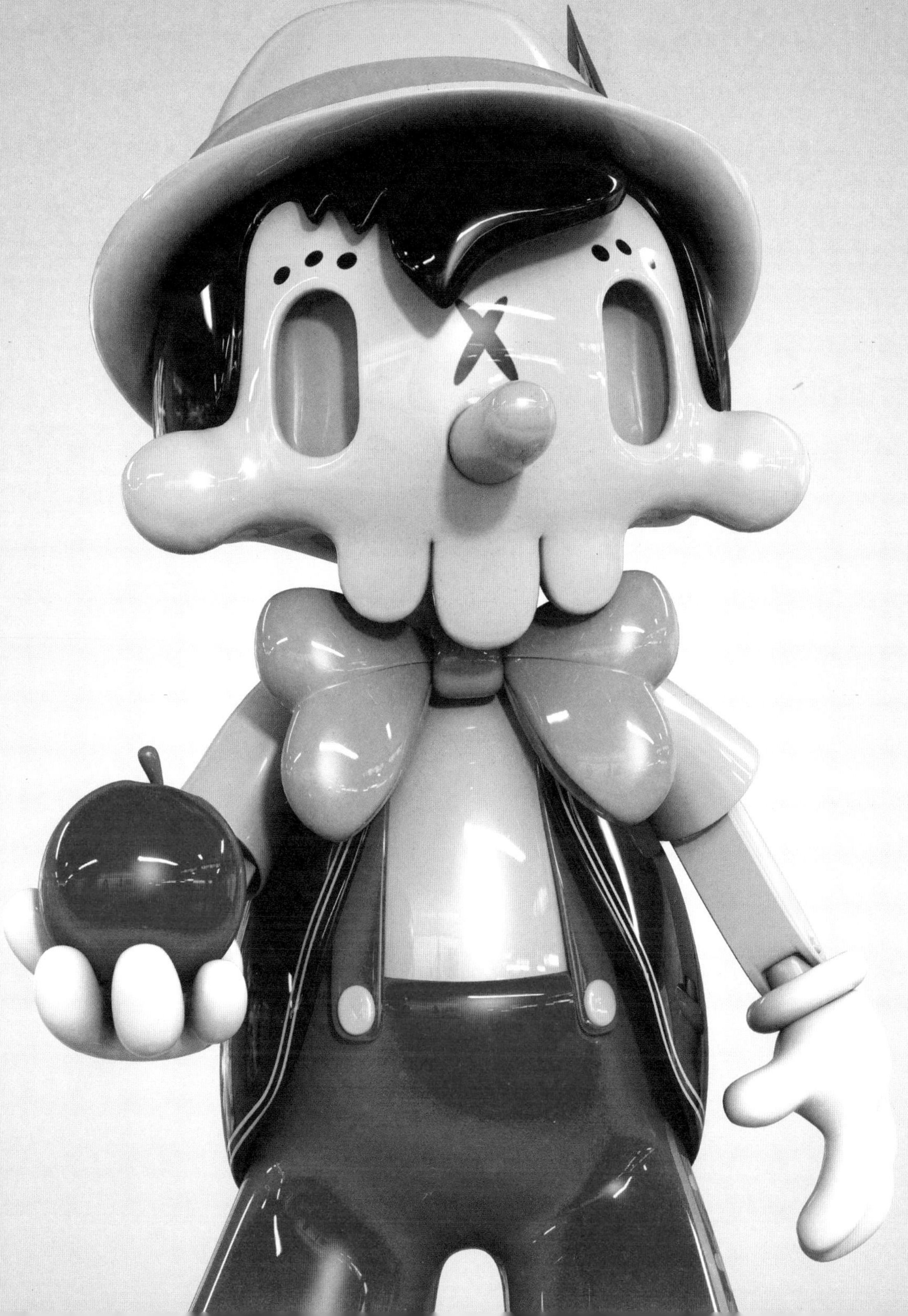

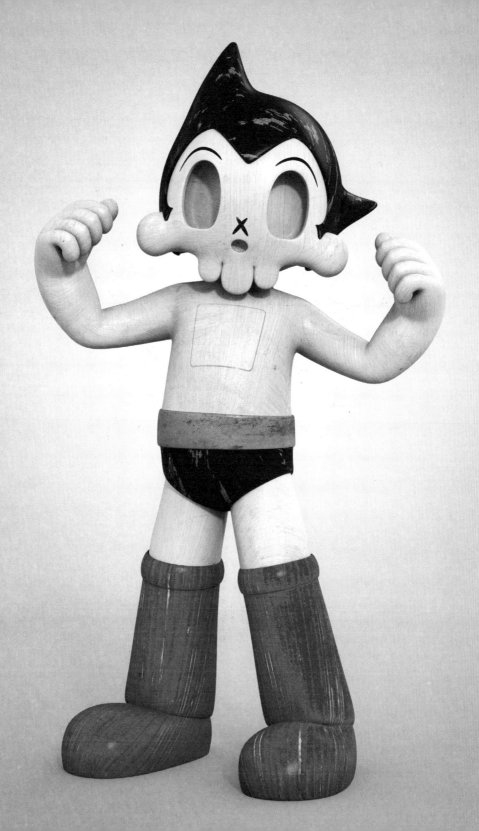

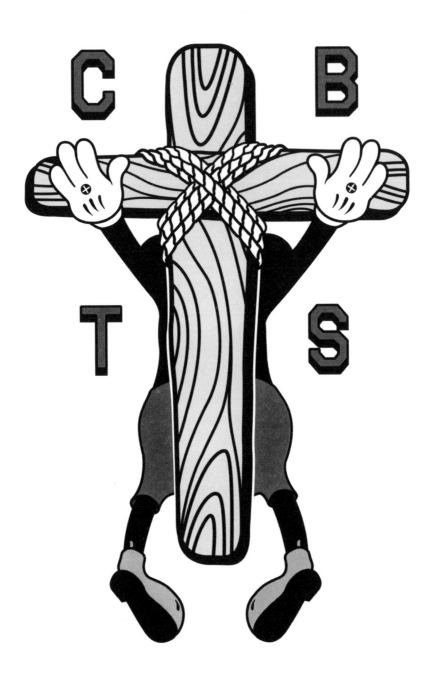

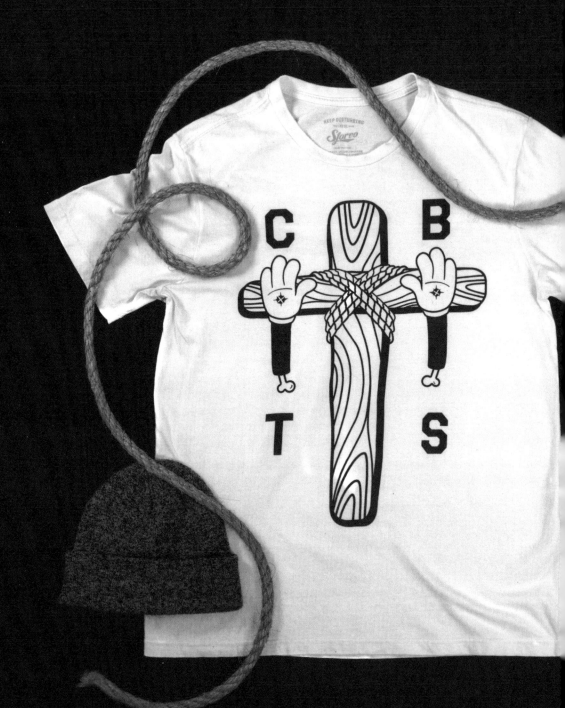

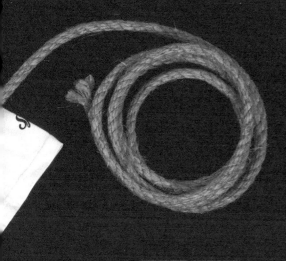

CRUCIFIED
BY THE
SYSTEM

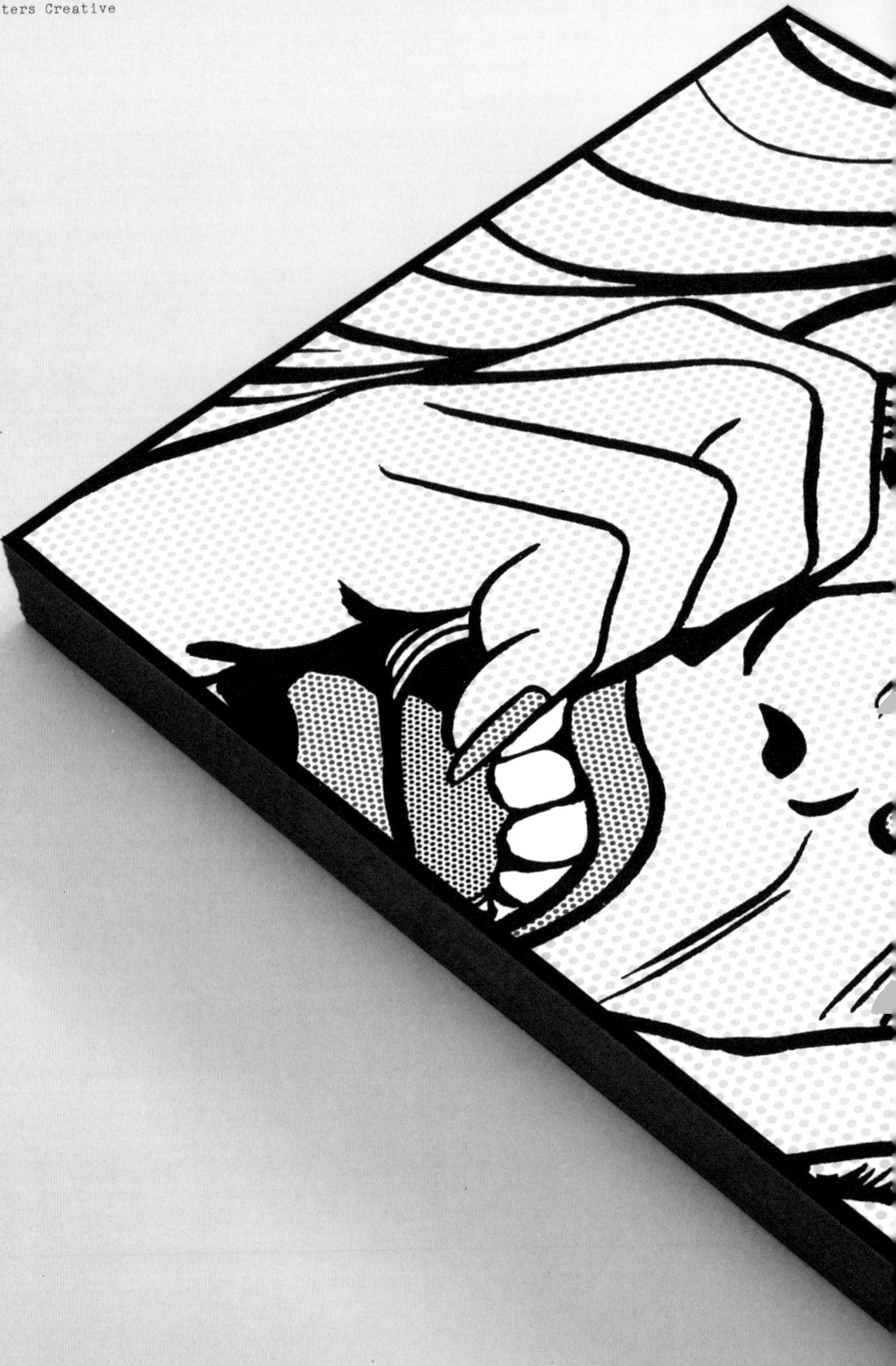

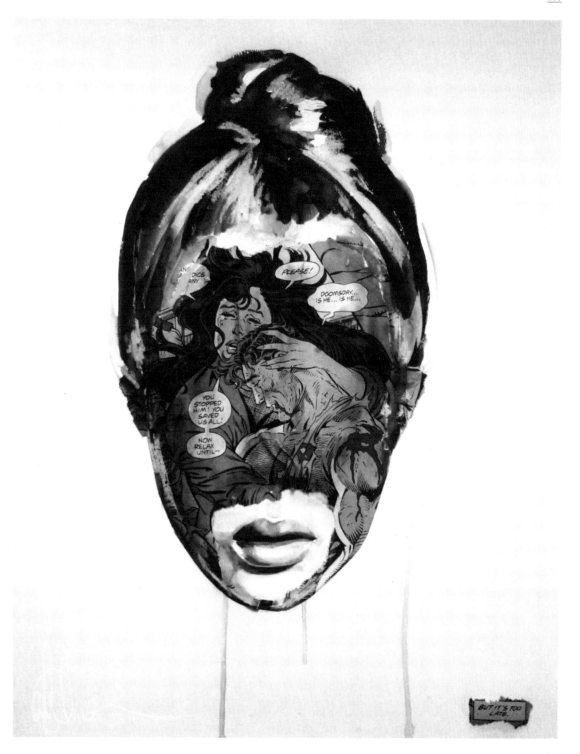

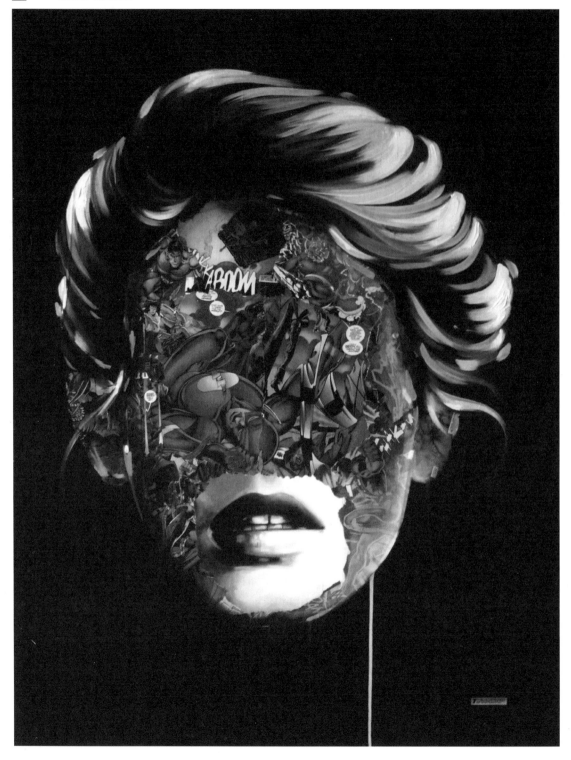

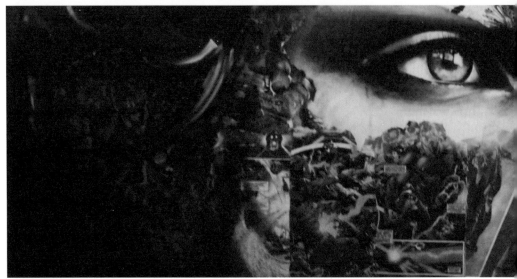

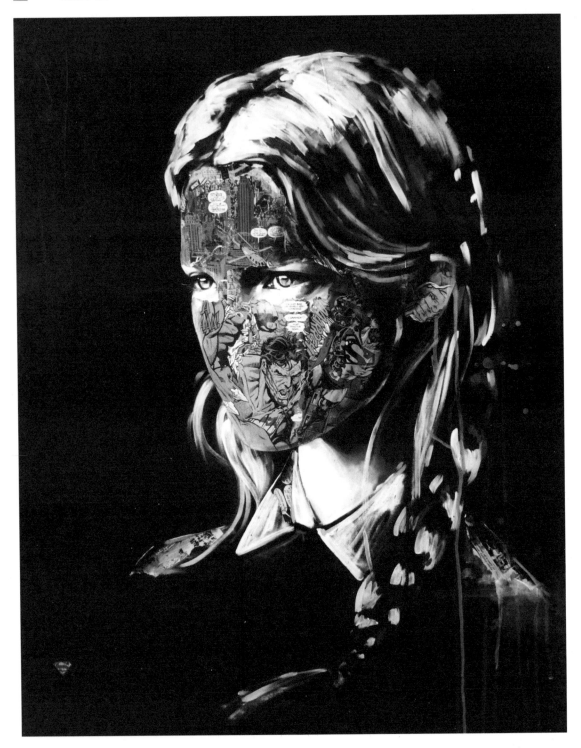

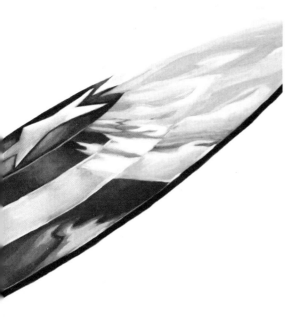

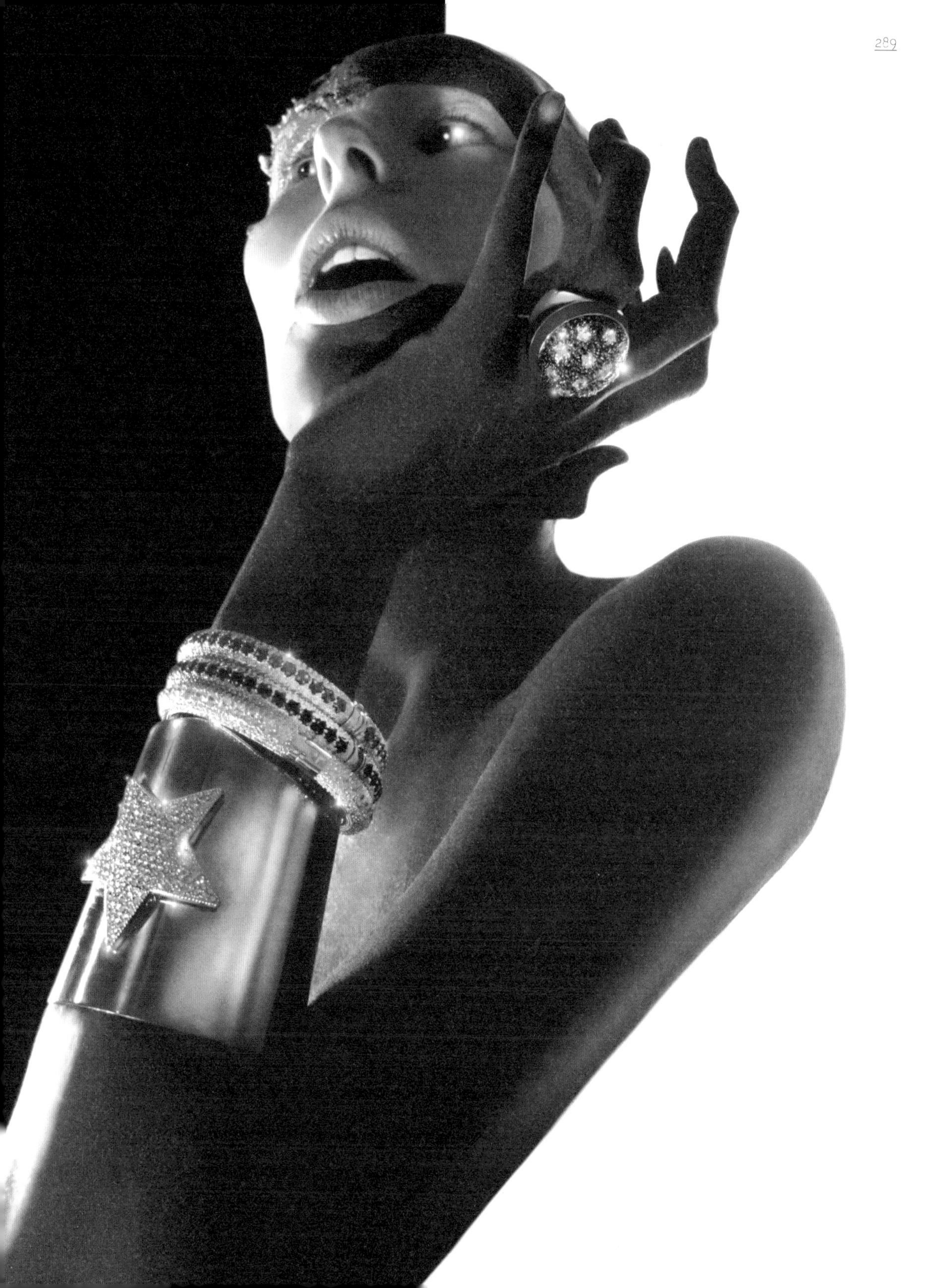

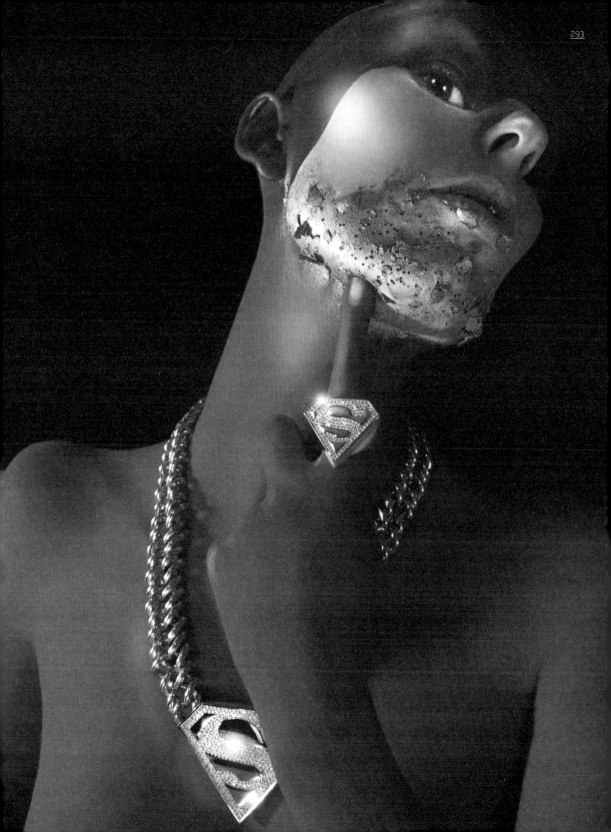

GET PERSONAL WITH 12 STAR ARTISTS WHO LET SUPERHEROES AND CHILDHOOD CLASSICS POP BEYOND THE FRAMES AND SCREENS. FROM THE WEST AND THE EAST, THESE ARTISTS OPEN THEIR HEART AND TALK ABOUT THEIR LOVE-HATE RELATIONSHIPS WITH CARTOONS AND MANGA, AND WHAT THEY WILL DO NEXT.

BEYOND THE FRAMES

DIALOGUE WITH...

BEN FROST!

PROFILE

All that looks wonderfully pleasing, jolly, and worthy of trust on food and medical packaging reveals a darker side when Australian postmodern pop artist Ben Frost puts satirical cartoons or erotic manga next to these classic advertising vocabularies. These empty fries, cereal and pharmaceutical boxes remaining of our consumer culture become the perfect medium for Frost to flaunt his wicked sense of humour and comment on modern lifestyle.

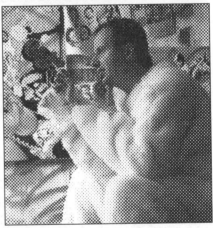

WHAT DO YOU LOVE ABOUT POP CULTURE? WHY DO YOU THINK IT IS EFFECTIVE TO GET YOUR IDEAS ACROSS THROUGH THIS MEDIUM?

I HAVE A LOVE/HATE RELATIONSHIP WITH POPULAR CULTURE. I'M ALWAYS TRYING TO SEE BEHIND THE FAÇADE OF THE COLOURFUL CHARACTERS, ICONS AND LOGOS THAT COMPANIES AND ADVERTISERS PRESENT TO US FOR THEIR DEEPER AND MORE OMINOUS MOTIVATIONS. POPULAR CULTURE IS SOMETHING WE ALL SHARE ON SOME LEVEL AND SO IN MY ARTWORK I RE-USE THE ELEMENTS WE SEE NEARLY EVERY DAY ON TELEVISION AND THE INTERNET, AS A CONCEPTUAL AND CREATIVE ENTRY POINT TO COMMUNICATE IDEAS.

WHAT IS YOUR FAVOURITE GRAPHIC NOVEL OR ANIMATED CARTOON? WHY IS IT SPECIAL TO YOU?

GROWING UP, I WAS ALWAYS A FAN OF BRITISH COMIC "2000AD". JUDGE DREDD, SLÁINE, ABC WARRIORS, CHOPPER, FUTURE SHOCKS, STRONTIUM DOG, NEMESIS THE WARLOCK, ZENITH, ROGUE TROOPER BLEW MY LITTLE MIND EVERY WEEK. THERE WAS DEFINITELY A PERIOD IN THE LATE 80S AND EARLY 90S WHEN COMICS MOVED FROM THESE VISUALLY 'CLUNKY' BLACK AND WHITE STORIES INTO FULL COLOUR, OFTEN HAND-PAINTED AND ABSTRACTED DEPICTIONS OF THE CHARACTERS. I LOVED THE FUTURISTIC STORIES OF "2000AD" MIXED WITH DARK HUMOUR, AND THE WAY THEY REFLECTED THE SOCIETY OF THE TIME.

HOW DIFFERENT IN YOUR OPINION IS TODAY'S PORTRAYAL OF POP CULTURE THAN IT WAS 20 YEARS AGO?

OUR RELATIONSHIP WITH POP CULTURE HAS BECOME MORE OBSESSIVE BUT AT THE SAME TIME MORE DISPOSABLE. THERE'S ALWAYS ANOTHER TV DOWNLOAD, TOY, OR T-SHIRT THAT YOU JUST 'HAVE TO HAVE' — BUT 15 MINUTES LATER YOU'LL FORGET ABOUT THAT AND ARE PRESENTED WITH THE NEXT OBJECT OF DISTRACTION. ART AND DESIGN HAVE BECOME LIKE THAT NOW AND I THINK IT HAS A LOT TO DO WITH THE EXPLOSION OF PEOPLE WHO HAVE BECOME INVOLVED IN THE CREATIVE ARTS.

WHAT DO ANIME AND MANGA ADD TO YOUR WORK? HOW IS IT DIFFERENT FROM WORKING WITH WESTERN COMICS AND CARTOONS?

MANGA AND HENTAI HAVE THIS DUALITY BETWEEN CUTENESS AND AGGRESSION THAT WORKS WELL IN MY PAINTINGS. THE CHARACTERS MIGHT BE DEPICTED DOING HORRIFIC THINGS LIKE CUTTING OFF PEOPLE'S HEADS OR HAVING SEX WITH TENTACLE MONSTERS — BUT THEY RETAIN A SENSE OF COMIC INNOCENCE ON THE SURFACE THAT MAKES WHAT THEY'RE DOING LESS 'REAL'. WESTERN COMICS — WHILE STILL INVOLVED IN FANTASY ARE ALWAYS ATTEMPTING TO DEPICT A SENSE OF REALITY BOTH VISUALLY AND CONCEPTUALLY.

YOUR WORK IS LAYERED WITH GRAPHIC ELEMENTS ACROSS DISCIPLINES AND CULTURES. HOW DO YOU MASH THEM UP TOGETHER INTO A SINGLE PIECE OF WORK? ARE ALL RESULTS PLANNED OR SHAPED AS YOU CREATE?

THE MASH-UP STYLE OF PAINTING THAT I DO IS THE MOST FUN. THE PROCESS INVOLVES COLLECTING LOTS AND LOTS OF IMAGES AND FROM THERE I USE AN OVERHEAD PROJECTOR (LIKE THE OLD ONES WE USED TO HAVE IN SCHOOLS) TO COMPOSE AND START PAINTING THE LAYERS. IT CAN BE VERY FRUSTRATING SOMETIMES BECAUSE WHEN SOMETHING HAS BEEN PAINTED ONTO THE CANVAS, THERE'S NO 'UNDO' BUTTON SO THE LAYERS BECOME MORE AGGRESSIVE — ALMOST AS IF THEY'RE COMPETING WITH EACH OTHER TO BE SEEN. IN THIS WAY I CAN'T BE TOO RIGOROUS ABOUT THE WORK — IF SOMETHING I'VE SPENT HOURS PAINTING GETS COVERED WITH DRIPS OR ANOTHER LAYER, THEN THAT'S JUST THE WAY IT IS. IT'S THE PROCESS THAT IS THE MOST ENJOYABLE TO ME AND BEING ABLE TO SEE HOW THE LAYERS CAME TOGETHER WHEN THE WORK IS DONE IS MUCH LIKE READING A STORY.

WHY DO YOU DRAW AND PAINT ON FOOD AND PHARMACEUTICAL PACKAGING? HOW DO THEY RELATE TO THE ILLUSTRATIONS DRAWN ON TOP OF THEM?

I THINK THERE'S A BIG DIFFERENCE BETWEEN ACTUALLY PAINTING A MCDONALD'S LOGO AND PAINTING ONTO A DISCARDED MCDONALD'S PACKAGE. THE LOGO STILL APPEARS IN THE ARTWORK SO THE DIALOGUE IS STILL RELATIVELY THE SAME BUT THE INTENTION CHANGES DRAMATICALLY. I WAS PHYSICALLY USING THE REFUSE THAT THE CORPORATIONS ARE FORCING UPON US AND 'RE-PURPOSING' THEM SO WE CAN LOOK AT THEM IN A NEW WAY. THE IMAGES I JUXTAPOSED ONTO THE PACKAGING WERE USU-

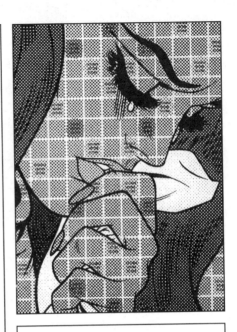

ALLY EITHER 'MELANCHOLIC': REFLECTING HOW 'WASTE' IS AFFECTING THE PLANET VIA IMAGERY OF INNOCENT CRYING WOMEN, OR AGGRESSIVE AND PORNOGRAPHIC HENTAI/MANGA IMAGERY TO REFLECT HOW WE'RE BEING TAKEN ADVANTAGE OF BY CONSUMERISM.

YOU REVEAL THE DARK SIDE OF NUMEROUS ANGELIC CARTOON CHARACTERS THROUGH IMAGERY OF SEX AND VIOLENCE. WHAT DO YOU WISH TO SAY HERE?

IT'S A REFLECTION OF OUR SOCIETY AND WHAT I CHOSE TO PICK UP ON FROM MY OBSERVATIONS OF ADVERTISING AND THE MEDIA. THE EXPERIENCE OF WATCHING TELEVISION OR BEING ON THE INTERNET IS AN EMOTIONAL ROLLER-COASTER RIDE OF UPS AND DOWNS, FEAR AND EXCITEMENT AND THESE CONTRASTING ELEMENTS ARE CONSTANTLY BEING FED TO US IN SUCCESSION. IT'S LIKE WE'RE SWIMMING IN AN 'IMAGE SOUP' AND ALL THE ELEMENTS ARE SWIRLING TOGETHER AND NEXT TO EACH OTHER IN OFTEN DISTURBING AND DISTASTEFUL WAYS.

YOUR WORK HAS BEEN EXHIBITED AROUND THE WORLD. HOW DO YOU PERCEIVE SOME OF THE MORE RADICAL RESPONSES FROM VIEWERS?

I'M ALWAYS SURPRISED HOW DE-SENSITISED PEOPLE ARE TO SOME OF THE MORE GRAPHIC IMAGES THAT I USE IN MY WORK. I THINK IF YOU USE CONFRONTING IMAGES IN A CLEVER OR WELL-THOUGHT OUT WAY, THEN IT DOESN'T COME ACROSS AS SO OFFENSIVE.

WHAT IS THE MOST CHALLENGING ASPECT OF YOUR APPROACH? HOW DID YOU GET IT SORTED OUT?

MY PROCESS INVOLVES SPENDING A LOT OF TIME FIND-ING IMAGES THAT I CAN SUBVERT AND PLAY WITH — SO I GUESS THAT'S THE MOST TIME-CONSUMING PRO-CESS. FROM THERE IT BECOMES ALL ABOUT COMPOSI-TION, AND HOW I CAN CHANGE THE IMAGES TO CREATE NEW DIALOGUES. I ENJOY THE IDEA OF ATTRACTION VER-SUS REPULSION — SO I'M ALWAYS TRYING TO JUXTAPOSE CUTE IMAGES WITH HORRIFIC IMAGES. THIS IS WHAT I THINK THE WORLD IS LIKE EVERY TIME YOU TURN ON THE TELEVISION — A CONSTANT BARRAGE OF OPPOSING AND EMOTIONALLY CONTRASTING PICTURES AND THEMES.

WHAT ARE YOU PLANNING ON DOING NEXT? IS THERE SOMETHING YOU'RE EAGER TO EXPLORE?

I'VE BEEN PAINTING ONTO FOUND PACKAGES FOR A FEW YEARS NOW AND I'M ALWAYS FINDING NEW AND INTERESTING THINGS TO PAINT ONTO. I'VE RECENTLY BEEN USING BOARD GAMES, CHILDREN'S BED SHEETS, MORTUARY TOE TAGS AND VINTAGE STAMPS — BUT THERE'RE ALWAYS NEW THINGS THAT I FIND ON MY TRAV-ELS THAT SPARK NEW INTEREST. I LIKE THE IDEA THAT I'M 'RECYCLING' THE OBJECT AND ALSO WHEN IT HAS SOME PERSONAL ASSOCIATION WHETHER TO ME OR TO THE VIEWER — WHICH I THINK HAS MORE INHERENT POWER THAN SOMETHING PAINTED ONTO A CANVAS.

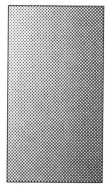

DIALOGUE WITH...

BENOIT LAPRAY!

PROFILE

A background in advertising photography and photo retouching, and a fondness for nature induce French artist Benoit Lapray to remind us that superheroes actually have a human side. Despite gifted with exceptional talents to fight crimes and adored by humans, they feel lonesome at times and remain insignificant in front of nature - the part of life often missed out in the movies. Currently a photo retoucher in commercial photography, Lapray is keen to bring familiar fictional characters to real life and provoke deeper thoughts into their life.

WHAT DO COMICS MEAN TO YOU? WHY DO YOU THINK IT IS EFFECTIVE TO GET IDEAS ACROSS THROUGH THIS MEDIUM?

FOR ME COMICS MEAN: IMAGINATION, CREATIVITY, FANTASY... AND ALSO REALITY. I THINK IT WAS AND IT IS ONE OF THE BEST WAY FOR SOMEONE TO EXPRESS HIMSELF. PROBABLY MORE THAN PAINTING, PHOTOGRAPHY, CINEMA, LITERATURE...

COMICS' AUTHORS DEAL WITH REALITY AND REAL EVENTS, BUT THEY IMAGINE SUPERNATURAL THINGS TO SHOW THE BRAVERY WE CAN HAVE TO FIGHT INJUSTICE AND ALL BAD

THINGS THAT TAKE PLACE IN OUR WORLD. AND WITH THEIR ILLUSTRATED STORIES THEY EXPRESS ALL FRUSTRATIONS AND HOPES OF A GENERATION.

HOW DID "THE QUEST FOR THE ABSOLUTE" BEGIN?

WELL, THIS SERIES STARTED IN MY MIND WHILE I WAS WALKING IN THE MOUNTAINS (IN HAUTE-SAVOIE IN THE FRENCH ALPS, WHERE I LIVED FOR FIVE YEARS BETWEEN 2006 AND 2011). AT THE BEGINNING THE SERIES WAS JUST A GAME. AND THEN IT BECAME A WORK I IMPOSED MYSELF ON. IT STARTED WITH A PICTURE OF SUPERMAN. I HAD THE IDEA TO PUT HIM ON A BIG ROCK BALANCED IN THE AIR, AND IT WORKED IMMEDIATELY. THE RESULT WAS REALLY POWERFUL. SO I REALISED THAT THERE WAS AN EVIDENT LINK BETWEEN SUPERHEROES AND NATURE. NORMALLY SUPERHERO STORIES TAKE PLACE IN BIG CITIES, HOWEVER IN NATURE IT ALSO WORKED VERY WELL.

WHY DO YOU THINK "THE ABSOLUTE" CAN BE FOUND IN THE NATURE?

WELL, IT IS NOT EXACTLY WHAT I WANT TO EXPRESS WITH THIS SERIES. IN FACT IT IS JUST A HYPOTHESIS, BUT I GUESS THAT THE ABSOLUTE CAN BE FOUND NOT 'IN' THE NATURE BUT 'WITH' NATURE. SO FOR ME, IN MY STORY, NATURE IS A CHARACTER, LIKE THE SUPERHEROES. AND THEY STARTED A QUEST, TOGETHER, TO SUCCEED AND TO REACH THE ABSOLUTE. I LIKE THIS IDEA.

THESE SUPERHEROES LOOK ISOLATED AND INSIGNIFICANT IN THE PICTURES — VERY DIFFERENT FROM HOW THEY ARE DEPICTED IN COMICS. WHAT ARE YOU TRYING TO PORTRAY THROUGH THESE CHARACTERS?

INDEED IN MY PICTURES SUPERHEROES LOOK INSIGNIFICANT COMPARED TO NATURE. IT IS TO STRESS THE FACT THAT EVEN A SUPERHERO IS A LITTLE THING COMPARED TO NATURE. SUPERHEROES AS HUMAN BEINGS ARE JUST A PART OF IT. IN A WAY NATURE IS EVERYTHING. SO I THINK IT WAS NORMAL TO SHOW THEM LIKE THAT.

WHERE ARE THESE SITES? WHAT TOOK YOU TO SHOOT PICTURES AT THESE SITES?

MOST SITES APPEARING IN MY SERIES ARE IN FRANCE, IN THE ALPS. BUT I ALSO SHOT PICTURES IN OTHER REGIONS OF MY COUNTRY. EACH TIME I GO FOR A WALK IN THE MOUNTAINS OR IN THE COUNTRYSIDE I TAKE MY CAMERA WITH ME AND SHOT SITES THAT I THINK ARE IMPRESSIVE, AND WHERE NATURE IS LUSH AND BEAUTIFUL.

WAS IT INTENTIONAL THAT YOU PICKED ONLY AMERICAN COMICS CHARACTERS FOR THE PROJECT? WHAT DO THEY MEAN TO YOU?

I CAN EASILY EXPLAIN THAT. IT IS JUST BECAUSE I KNOW MORE AMERICAN CHARACTERS THAN CHARACTERS FROM OTHER COUNTRIES. AND IT WAS ALSO BETTER TO KEEP A KIND OF UNITY TO THIS WORK.

WHAT IS THE MOST CHALLENGING ASPECT OF YOUR APPROACH? WERE YOU ON SOME OTHER PROJECTS AS WELL DURING THESE FOUR YEARS?

WHEN I STARTED THIS SERIES I WAS A FULL TIME PHOTOGRAPHER AT AN ADVERTISING PHOTO STUDIO, SO IT TOOK ME A LOT OF TIME, NEXT TO MY JOB, TO DEVELOP THIS WORK. AND I SHOT SEVERAL SERIES AT THE SAME TIME (WANDERING SPIRITS,

WILD INSTINCT, TOYS INVASION... THAT YOU CAN SEE ON MY WEBSITE: WWW.BENOITLAPRAY.COM). THAT IS WHY IT TOOK ME SO LONG TO DO IT. AND IT IS NOT OVER YET. THE SERIES IS STILL IN PROGRESS.

WHAT IS YOUR FAVOURITE COMICS OR CARTOON? WHY IS IT SPECIAL TO YOU?

I LIKE CHARACTERS OF COMICS BUT I DON'T REALLY READ IT. SO IT'S DIFFICULT TO TALK ABOUT MY FAVOURITE COMICS. BUT CONVERSELY I LIKE CARTOONS VERY MUCH. AND MY FAVOURITE CARTOON IS SOMETHING COMPLETELY DIFFERENT FROM STORIES OF SUPERHEROES. IT IS "LE ROI ET L'OISEAU (THE KING AND THE MOCKING BIRD)" BY PAUL GRIMAULT. I LIKE THE DRAWING OF THIS CARTOON AND THE POETIC

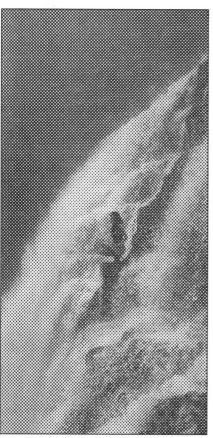

LANGUAGE OF THE STORY. YOU DON'T KNOW IF YOU ARE IN THE PAST OR THE FUTURE, AND THE TOPICS ARE UNIVERSAL: THE GOOD, THE BAD, LOVE, POWER, VANITY, JUSTICE... EVERYTHING IS DEVELOPED WITH SIMPLICITY. I SAW THESE CARTOONS WHEN I WAS YOUNG — THAT IS PROBABLY WHY I HAD A VERY SPECIAL FEELING WHEN I WATCH THEM, EVEN NOW.

WHAT ARE YOU PLANNING ON DOING NEXT? IS THERE SOMETHING YOU'RE EAGER TO EXPLORE?

I HAVE A LOT OF PROJECTS IN MY MIND, BUT THE NEXT ONE WILL PROBABLY BE A SERIES WITH PEOPLE IN THE STREETS OF A BIG CITY. I WOULD LIKE TO FOCUS MY NEXT WORK ON SOMETHING I LIKE TO ANALYSE: THE ENERGY WE CAN BRING INTO US. I WANT TO SHOW, ON PICTURES, THE ENERGY THAT EMANATES FROM PEOPLE. SO IT WILL BE A MIX BETWEEN STREET PHOTOGRAPHY AND SCENE, WITH A SPECIAL LIGHT SHOWING THE ENERGY OF INDIVIDUALS... WELL, THAT IS THE IDEA, BUT I STILL HAVE TO THINK THROUGH.

IF YOU WERE TO BECOME A SUPERHERO, WHAT SUPERPOWER DO YOU POSSESS?

AHAH! THAT IS A GOOD QUESTION. I THINK I WOULD BE PERFECT IN SUPERMAN. ALL HIS SUPERPOWERS ARE REALLY COOL. AND IF I COULD RUN REALLY FAST, FLY, AND RAISE UP MOUNTAINS, MY DAILY LIFE WOULD BE DEFINITELY DIFFERENT FOR SURE.

DIALOGUE WITH... BUTCHER BILLY!

PROFILE

Pop culture has prompted Butcher Billy to become a designer who, in return, adds merry fuel to the movement, blending personal fascinations and references from the 80s and 90s when he spent most of his adolescence watching television and playing video games. But this Brazilian creative director has a wider range of superheroes in mind. Iconic figures like Robert Smith, Salvador Dalí, and Roy Lichtenstein also significantly shaped who he is today.

WHAT DO YOU LOVE ABOUT COMICS? WHY DO YOU THINK IT IS EFFECTIVE TO GET YOUR IDEAS ACROSS THROUGH THIS MEDIUM?

I GUESS IT'S NOT ONLY COMICS, BUT REALLY THE SUPER-HERO CONCEPT THAT HAS BEEN INSERTED INTO THE POP CULTURE IN GENERAL MEANS EVERYTHING TO ME, WHEN THAT STARTED SHAPING MY INTEREST IN CINEMA, MUSIC, GAMES, COMICS, TV AND ART SINCE CHILDHOOD — ROBERT SMITH, SALVADOR DALÍ, JOHNNY ROTTEN, ANDY WARHOL, ROY LICHTENSTEIN — THEY ALL HAVE ALWAYS BEEN AS ICONIC TO ME AS SPIDER-MAN OR HULK, AND ALL OF THEM INSPIRE ME IN A WAY OR THE OTHER. I COULD SAY THAT POP CULTURE IS MAINLY THE REASON WHY I CHOSE TO BE A DESIGNER IN THE FIRST PLACE. THERE'S STILL A GENERAL IDEA THAT COMICS AND GAMES ARE MADE FOR CHILDREN. THAT CAN BE RIGHT AND SO WRONG AT THE SAME TIME, SO I LIKE TO ADD SOME GROWN-UP THEMES TO IT, LIKE POLITICS, SUICIDAL OR DEPRESSIVE ICONS AND ALL SORTS OF SARCASTIC REMARKS.

60¢
U.R. 20p
ALL NEW!
(MORE PAGES)
NO. 197
DEC.

THE CONCEPT OF 'FICTION VERSUS REALITY' PREVAILS YOUR WORK. WHAT DO THEY MEAN TO YOU?

I'VE ALWAYS BEEN A BIG FAN OF CINEMA, GAMES, COMICS, MUSIC, TV AND ARTS, BUT ALSO AN OBSERVER. I REMEMBER BEING JUST A LITTLE BOY AND READING MUSIC INDUSTRY MAGAZINES — I DIDN'T EVEN KNOW THE MUSIC BUT I WAS INTERESTED IN THE STORIES, LIFESTYLE AND EVERYTHING ABOUT THAT WORLD. I GUESS I WAS ALWAYS FASCINATED BY CULT ICONS — THE WAY THEY CAN BE LARGER THAN LIFE. MORE THAN JUST NORMAL PEOPLE BY BECOMING CHARACTERS IN PEOPLE'S MINDS. SO TO START MASHING THEM UP WITH ACTUAL FICTIONAL CHARACTERS WAS A VERY NATURAL THING.

IN "WAR PHOTOGRAPHY X VINTAGE COMICS", YOU MADE A NOTE THAT IN CONTRARY TO THE PROJECT, THE WORLD OF COMICS IS BLACK AND WHITE IN A METAPHORIC WAY, BUT IN THE REAL WORLD IT'S HARD FOR YOU TO DRAW A LINE BETWEEN *GOOD* AND *EVIL*. HOW DO YOU FEEL ABOUT THE ABSENCE OF GREY AREAS IN AMERICAN COMICS?

I BELIEVE THERE WERE TIMES WHEN COMICS WERE A LOT MORE TIED TO GOVERNMENT MARKETING INTERESTS, BUT FORTUNATELY THIS IS HISTORY NOW. COMICS SHOULD INSPIRE PEOPLE AND MAKE THEM THINK, NOT TURN THEM INTO IDIOTS.

WHAT'S YOUR CRITERIA FOR THE PAIRING OF MUSICIANS AND SUPERHEROES IN "THE POST-PUNK/ NEW WAVE SUPER FRIENDS"?

WELL, I FIRST HAD THE IDEA OF DRAWING MORRISSEY AS SUPERMAN — BECAUSE OF THE GLASSES, THE CHIN AND THE 'S' THAT COULD EASILY STAND FOR 'SMITHS' — HIS BAND — IF SEEN IN THAT WAY, NOT TO MENTION THE STATUS OF SANCTITY THAT MOZ SEEMS TO ELICIT IN PEOPLE — THAT WOULD MATCH NOT ONLY THE VISUAL ASPECT OF IT BUT ALSO THE PSYCHOLOGICAL. THEN I REALISED I COULD

EXPAND THAT IDEA INTO A FULL PROJECT, SINCE IAN CURTIS' PERSONALITY STARTED MAKING SO MUCH SENSE AS BATMAN. FROM THAT TO A WHOLE JUSTICE LEAGUE OF POST-PUNK, IT WAS JUST A STEP.

WHAT IS THE MOST CHALLENGING ASPECT OF YOUR APPROACH? HOW DID YOU GET IT SORTED OUT?

IT USUALLY TAKES LONG TO FIGURE OUT THE RIGHT TAKE TO THE CONCEPT OF A PROJECT, BUT I'M ACTUALLY INTERESTED IN THE IDEAS THAT ARE REALLY SIMPLE. AS SIMPLE AND AS INGENIOUS AS THE ONES THAT MAKE PEOPLE THINK: "HOW CAN I NEVER THINK OF THAT BEFORE?" I GUESS THAT'S THE COMMON REACTION TO PIECES LIKE IDENTIFY-

ING IAN CURTIS AS BATMAN AND MORRISSEY AS SUPERMAN. THEY ARE MASHUPS OF TOTALLY OPPOSITE VISUAL SOURCES, BUT IN THE WEIRDEST WAY THEY MAKE TOTAL SENSE. THAT'S WHAT I'M TRYING TO ACHIEVE.

YOU TAKE GRAPHICAL REFERENCE MOSTLY FROM AMERICAN COMICS. DO YOU READ ASIAN COMICS TOO? WHAT DO YOU THINK OF THEM?

IT'S FUNNY BECAUSE I VERY MUCH APPRECIATE THE STYLE OF ASIAN COMICS, ESPECIALLY THE VINTAGE ONES, LIKE OSAMU TEZUKA'S WORK, AND I LIKE TO THINK I'M INFLUENCED IN ONE WAY OR THE OTHER. IT'S JUST THAT I GREW UP READING AMERICAN COMICS, SO THAT SIDE SEEMS TO BE MORE PRESENT. BUT ON THE OTHER HAND THE ASIAN VINTAGE GAMES WERE A HUGE PART OF MY LIFE AND YOU CAN SEE A LOT OF THAT IN MY WORK.

WHAT IS YOUR FAVOURITE GRAPHIC NOVEL OR ANIMATED CARTOON? WHY IS IT SPECIAL TO YOU?

I WAS MOST CERTAINLY SHAPED BY THE CLASSICS, LIKE THE KILLING JOKE, THE DARK KNIGHT RETURNS, WATCHMEN, ARKHAM ASYLUM... CURRENTLY I'VE BEEN READING COMPILATIONS WITH THE VERY FIRST HELLBLAZER STORIES PUBLISHED AS MY MOST FAVOURITE CHARACTER OF ALL, JOHN CONSTANTINE, WRITTEN BY JAMIE DELANO. BUT DEFINITELY THE GRAPHIC NOVEL THAT HAD THE BIGGEST IMPACT ON ME IS FOR SURE "KINGDOM COME". IT WAS THE FIRST COMIC BOOK THAT BROUGHT A TEAR TO MY EYE. LATER ON, THINKING ABOUT IT, I REALISED HOW NERDY I WAS AND DECIDED TO GET A GIRLFRIEND.

HOW DIFFERENT IN YOUR OPINION IS TODAY'S PORTRAYAL OF POP CULTURE THAN IT WAS 20 YEARS AGO?

I'M AFRAID IT'S DEFINITELY MORE BORING NOW THAN IN THE 80S AND 90S. I WAS ONLY A KID BACK THEN BUT I RECALL IT BEING A LOT MORE FUN AND CYNICAL AND SARCASTIC AND CREATIVE. POLITICAL CORRECTNESS HAS DEFINITELY GONE MAD NOWADAYS — SEEMS LIKE THERE'S ALWAYS SOMEONE SUPER-OFFENDED WITH JUST ABOUT ANYTHING RELEVANT ANYONE ATTEMPTS TO SAY. PROBABLY THAT'S WHY SOME OF MY PROJECTS ARE LABELLED AS PROVOCATIVE OR CONTROVERSIAL.

IF YOU WERE TO BECOME A SUPERHERO, WHOM WILL YOU BE AND WHAT SUPERPOWER DO YOU POSSESS?

I WOULD LOVE TO HAVE SUPERMAN'S POWERS AND BATMAN'S INTELLECT AND RESOURCES — BUT WHO AM I KIDDING? I'VE ALWAYS BEEN MORE OF A JOHN CONSTANTINE KIND OF GUY.

WHAT ARE YOU PLANNING ON DOING NEXT? IS THERE SOMETHING YOU'RE EAGER TO EXPLORE?

SO MANY IDEAS AND SO LITTLE TIME TO DEVELOP THEM. I'VE BEEN LOOKING BACK AT THE 90S A LOT FOR INSPIRATION LATELY. I BELIEVE I'VE EXPLORED A LOT OF THE POST-PUNK SCENE OF THE 80S AND NOW I'VE BEEN VERY INTERESTED IN THE ACID HOUSE THAT CAME AFTER. YOU CAN EXPECT SOME OF THAT BEEN RELEASED FROM ME THIS YEAR (2014).

DIALOGUE WITH...
CHRIS PANDA!

PROFILE

Having attended University of Cali-
fornia, Los Angeles and currently
based in Paris, young French illustrator Chris Panda has been re-
lentlessly honing his illustration
skills, examining structures and
proportions that essentially make
drawn subjects real to life. "Xray"
is a by-product of one of his ex-
ercises where Chris Panda imagined
the odd bone structures within ficti-
tious characters, and made fascinat-
ing discoveries along the way. Chris
Panda's work also contains pinups
and pop costume highlights.

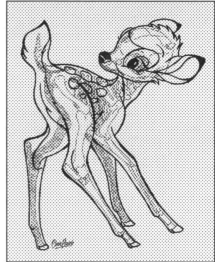

WHAT DO YOU LOVE ABOUT COMICS AND CAR-TOONS?

AS SIMPLE AS I WAS BORN IN THE 80S WHERE THE COMICS AND CARTOONS GENERALLY HAD EXPLODED IN TELEVISION, BOOKS AND ALL, SO I JUST BASICALLY FOLLOWED THE WAVES WHICH BROUGHT THAT NEW POP CULTURE AND FELL IN LOVE WITH THOSE SUPERHEROES, ROBOT, NINJA TURTLE OR WHATEVER THAT CAME TO ME.

WHY DO YOU THINK IT IS EFFECTIVE TO GET YOUR IDEAS ACROSS THROUGH THIS MEDIUM?

COMICS AND CARTOONS ARE NOW A BIG PART OF THE POP CULTURE. MY GENERATION BORN IN THE 80S HAS GROWN

UP WITH A HUGE AMOUNT OF QUALITY CARTOON AND COMICS AND WITH THE EXPLOSION OF THE SUPERHERO INDUSTRY, SOME CARTOON COMPANIES SUCH AS DISNEY, PIXAR, DREAMWORKS, ETC. HAVE BECOME A HANDY MEANS TO SPEAK TO KIDS, TEENAGERS AND ADULTS. SO FOR ME IT'S DEFINITELY THE BEST WAY TO MAKE WHAT I LOVE AND SPEAK TO THE MOST PEOPLE.

WHAT TAKES YOU TO CREATE YOUR "XRAY" SERIES? WHAT DO YOU LOVE ABOUT BONES AND SKELETONS?

"XRAY" WASN'T MEANT TO BE A SERIES AT THE BEGINNING... I ONLY PLANNED TO START EXERCISING DRAWING AND EX-AMINE HOW THE BEST CARTOON ILLUSTRATORS IMAGINE THE STRUCTURE OF A CHARACTER AND PEOPLE STARTED TO GO COMPLETELY CRAZY ABOUT IT. AFTER THAT I JUST DECIDED TO MAKE A WHOLE SERIES TO DEVELOP MY SKILLS AND FOR FUN, ENGENDERING SKELETONS FOR THE BEST CHARACTERS IN POP CULTURE.

I DO NOT KNOW IF I CAN SAY I LOVE BONES AND SKEL-ETONS, BUT I LOVE THE IDEA OF UNCOVERING WHAT'S HID-ING INSIDE THEM.

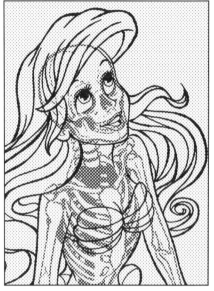

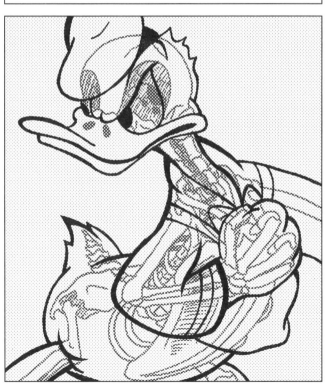

WHAT DO THESE SKELETAL STRUCTURES SAY ABOUT THESE COMICS AND CARTOON CHARACTERS IN YOUR SERIES?

SINCE THE BEGINNING I HAVE TRIED TO BE 100% ACCURATE AND FAITH-FUL ABOUT THE STRUCTURES, FOR EXAMPLE, HUMAN SKELETON FOR HUMAN OR ANIMAL SKELETON FOR ANIMAL CHARACTER... I HAVE STUD-IED THE SUBJECT A LOT TO WORK OUT THE SKELETON OF DIFFER-ENT SPECIES SO THOSE SKELETAL STRUCTURES WILL SHOW US HOW SOME CHARACTERS ARE REALLY WELL THOUGHT OUT AND LOOK AUTHENTICALLY HUMAN, WHEREAS SOME ARE COMPLETELY CRAZY AND UNREALISTIC, SUCH AS JES-SICA RABBIT AND BATMAN BY BRUCE TIMM.

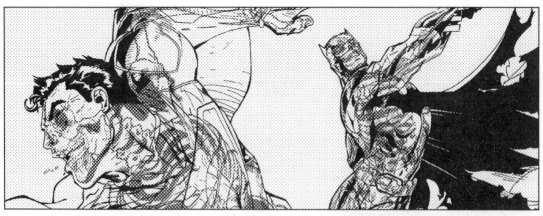

"XRAY" FEATURES QUITE A NUMBER OF WELL-KNOWN CARTOON CHARACTERS. WHY DO YOU PICK THEM? WHAT DO THEY MEAN TO YOU?

I PRINCIPALLY PICKED THEM BECAUSE THEY ARE MORE KNOWN TO EVERYONE AND THAT THEY ARE THE CHARACTERS I SAW AND FOLLOWED SINCE I WAS A CHILD. SO THEY ARE THE CHARACTERS I LOVE MOST IN THE COMICS/ CARTOON/ POP CULTURE.

CAN YOU TELL US SOMETHING ABOUT HOW YOU IMAGINE THE DIFFERENT BONE STRUCTURES? DO ALL SKELETONS SHARE MORE OR LESS THE SAME BASIC STRUCTURE?

AS I SAID BEFORE I NEVER IMAGINE A CRAZY UNREALISTIC SKELETON, I ALWAYS STUDY THE SKELETON SPECIES BEFORE DRAWING IT, AND WITH THAT I LEARN THAT A LOT OF SKELETON HAS GOT THE SAME BASIC STRUCTURE, AND AT THE END YOU UNDERSTAND MORE ABOUT HOW TO WORK THE BODY.

IF YOU WERE TO BECOME A SUPERHERO, WHAT SUPERPOWER DO YOU POSSESS?

BEING A SUPERHERO MEANS DOING SUPER THINGS, LIKE SAVING PEOPLE, FIGHTING VILLAINS AND ALSO I THINK IF I BECAME ONE I WOULD LIKE TO HAVE THE KIND OF POWER FROM WOLVERINE, SUCH AS HIS SUPERSTRENGTH, REGENERATIVE POWER, FIGHTING SKILLS, AND WHY NOT THE ADAMANTIUM SKELETON TO STAY ON THE XRAY MOOD HAHA!

WHAT IS THE MOST CHALLENGING ASPECT OF YOUR APPROACH? HOW DID YOU GET IT SORTED OUT?

THE MOST CHALLENGING ASPECT FOR ME IS TO REALISE A WORK THAT EVERYBODY WILL RECOGNISE AND APPRECIATE BUT SADLY I CAN DO NOTHING BEFORE SHOWING IT TO CHANGE THAT.

WHAT IS YOUR FAVOURITE GRAPHIC NOVEL OR ANIMATED CARTOON? WHY IS IT SPECIAL TO YOU?

IT'S A BIT HARD TO REPLY THAT ONE BUT IF I REALLY HAVE TO CHOOSE JUST ONE I THINK I WILL GO FOR THE "X-MEN" UNIVERSE AS THAT'S THE FIRST COMIC BOOK I EVER READ, AS SIMPLE AS THAT.

WHAT ARE YOU PLANNING ON DOING NEXT? IS THERE SOMETHING YOU'RE EAGER TO EXPLORE?

I WOULD WORK ON SOME GRAPHICAL ILLUSTRATION ABOUT THE FAMOUS SUITS OR COSTUMES IN POP CULTURE. BUT ABOVE THAT I WOULD HONE MY ILLUSTRATION SKILLS SO THAT I CAN HAVE MY OWN COMIC BOOK PUBLISHED ONE DAY.

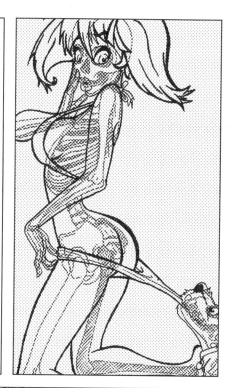

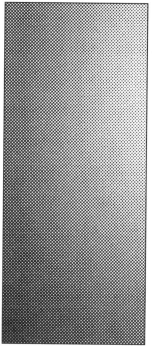

DIALOGUE WITH...
FANTASISTA UTAMARO!

WHAT DO YOU LOVE ABOUT ANIME AND MANGA? WHY DO YOU THINK IT IS EFFECTIVE TO GET YOUR IDEAS ACROSS THROUGH THIS MEDIUM?

I THINK THAT COMICS AND ANIME ARE JAPANESE ORIGINAL CULTURE AND I VERY MUCH BELIEVE THAT COMICS AND ANIME CULTURE IS VERY VERY IMPORTANT TO JAPANESE. THIS IS HOW WE DEVELOP OUR IDENTITY. I WANT TO TRY TO EXPAND ON AND SHOW THE WORLD THE POSSIBILITIES OF COMICS AND ANIME BECAUSE THEY ARE VERY INTERESTING. MANGA IS THE LOVE OF MY LIFE AND REASON FOR EXISTENCE. MANGA AND ANIME HAVE BECOME A PART OF ORDINARY LIFE IN JAPAN, ESPECIALLY TOKYO. I THINK ONCE

PROFILE

Manga art finds no boundaries in Fantasista Utamaro's eyes. If this vocabulary has brought enough drama in between the pages in black and white, Utamaro augments this influence with rich colours and patterns, as printed graphics and real life elements across photography, music videos and the fashion world. Hailed as an art director and designer in an environment steeped in manga art, Utamaro brings his ultra pop sensibilities to our visual culture with an explosive and fun energy unmistakably his own.

YOU STEP OUT OF THE PLANE IN JAPAN, YOU WILL FIND YOURSELF SO SURROUNDED BY MANGA AND ANIME WHICH IS A VERY VERY UNIQUE AND ODD SITUATION. BUT JAPANESE GET USED TO IT. THAT'S WHAT MAKES MANGA AND ANIME INTERESTING.

HOW WOULD YOU DESCRIBE YOUR GRAPHIC STYLE?

UNREALITY. BUT I'M STILL TRYING TO EXPLORE MYSELF AND ITS MEANING.

ONOMATOPOEIA HAS CREATED A LOT OF MUTED EXCITEMENT IN YOUR WORK. WHAT DOES IT MEAN TO YOU AND YOUR WORK?

IT IS THE SYMBOL OF WHAT I THINK OF JAPANESE CULTURE NOW. JAPANESE POP CULTURE IS THE CONTEXT WITHOUT IDENTITY. THIS IS SOMEHOW STEMMED IN BUDDHISM. BUDDHISM TELLS YOU ARE NOTHING AND EVERYTHING. I AM HE AS YOU ARE HE AS YOU ARE I, AND WE ARE ALL TOGETHER. SEE MY WORK THROUGH WHAT WE ARE AND COME FROM AND TELL ME WHAT IS JAPANESE. YOU WILL FIND THE EMPTINESS IN IT.

YOUR TYPOGRAPHY DESIGN IS ORGANIC, DYNAMIC AND DIVERSE. FROM WHERE DO YOU GET THE INSPIRATION?

MAYBE FROM MY CHILDHOOD. I AM NOT SURE WHERE MY INSPIRATION COME FROM. THE WORDS I PUT INTO MY DESIGN ARE SYMBOLS THAT STAND FOR JAPANESE CULTURE. THEY DO NOT MEAN ANYTHING BUT SOUNDS, BUT AT SAME TIME IT HAS CHARACTER IN IT.

NEON, SOFT TONES, BOLD TONES, SOLID PAINT-MIX-HALFTONE, WHITE LINES, BLACK LINES — WHAT DIFFERENCES CAN COLOURS CREATE IN MANGA GRAPHICS, ESPECIALLY IN YOUR TEXTILE DESIGN?

I AM COLOUR BLIND, BUT I THINK I AM AFFECTED BY THE VIEW OF AKIHABARA CITY WHERE SO MANY STORES CRAMMED INTO ONE PLACE.

THE COMPOSITION OF BOLD MANGA GRAPHICS AND REAL LIFE MODELS ARE ICONIC OF YOUR WORK. HOW DO YOU MAKE SURE THESE GRAPHICS STILL COMPOSE THE SAME IMPACT IN ACTUAL SPACE AND VOLUME AS THEY ARE IN THE BOOKS FROM INITIAL CONCEPT TO THE FINAL IMAGE??

THE CONCEPT IS DEVELOPED BASED ON THE FEELING OF WRONGNESS. I KEEP ENQUIRING INTO THE FEELING OF WRONGNESS THROUGH EXPERIMENTATIONS, AND FIND SOMETHING VERY NEW IN THAT AREA. IT IS VERY HARD TO EXPLAIN ABOUT THE FEELING THAT I HAVE.

HOW DIFFERENT IN YOUR OPINION IS TODAY'S PORTRAYAL OF POP CULTURE THAN IT WAS 20 YEARS AGO?

IT IS VERY CLEAR. IT IS MORE MIXED THAN EVER. ANIME, MANGA, MUSIC, AND FASHION ARE ALL MIXED WITH THE SPICE OF FANTASY AND THEY ARE VERY BALANCED.

DO YOU KEEP A SCRAPBOOK OR A COLLECTION OF THINGS FOR CREATIVE INSPIRATIONS? WHAT CAN BE FOUND IN YOUR COLLECTION?

I ALWAY HAVE MY SCRAPBOOK WITH ME. WHENEVER I COME UP THE IDEAS, I WRITE THEM DOWN. IT COULD BE WORDS OR ROUGH DRAWING.

WHAT WAS YOUR FIRST MANGA BOOK AND FAVOURITE GRAPHIC NOVEL ABOUT? WHAT WAS IT LIKE TURNING FROM A MANGA READER TO A MANGA CREATOR?

MY FIRST MANGA BOOK WAS "DR. SLUMP — ARALE-CHAN" BY AKIRA TORIYAMA, AND MY FAVOURITE'S "DRAGON BALL" BECAUSE IT IS FULL OF CREATIVE PHILOSOPHY. IT IS MY BIBLE!!! I WAS BORN TO BE CREATOR AND NEVER HAVE BEEN JUST A READER.

WHAT ARE YOU PLANNING ON DOING NEXT? IS THERE SOMETHING YOU'RE EAGER TO EXPLORE?

TURNING MY FOCUS FROM 2D TO 3D. I WANT TO TRY TO PAINT PICTURE SOMETHING BETWEEN VIRTUAL REALTY AND REALTY MIXING WITH IMAGINATION WORLD AND REAL WORLD.

DIALOGUE WITH...
LAZY OAF!

PROFILE

It all started out in 2001 in London where Gemma Shiel brought her great love for drawing and knowledge of textile design together as a small screen printer, and where her manufacture of handmade T-shirts for friends grew into a full fashion label as what we know as Lazy Oaf today. Lazy Oaf clothing is notoriously colourful, cartoon inspired, heavy on 90s nostalgia from her teenage years, and trendsetting with tongue-in-cheek humour. All graphics presented in her collections are hand drawn, occasionally adorned with lovely mistakes.

WHAT DO YOU LOVE ABOUT POP ART, COMICS AND CARTOONS? WHY DO YOU THINK IT IS EFFECTIVE TO GET YOUR IDEAS ACROSS THROUGH THIS MEDIUM?

I LOVE ALL OF THE ABOVE AS IT IS SO EASY TO ENGAGE AND RELATE TO. WHATEVER MESSAGE YOU ARE TRYING TO CONVEY THERE IS NO INTIMIDATION, THERE IS ALWAYS ELEMENTS OF FUN, COMEDY, PLAYFULNESS AND WIT ASSOCIATED WITH THESE GENRES. YOU CAN DIP IN AND OUT OF THESE ELEMENTS WITH EASE AND TAKE WHAT YOU WANT FROM THEM AND THAT IS WHAT APPEALS TO ME.

HOW DIFFERENT IN YOUR OPINION IS TODAY'S PORTRAYAL OF POP CULTURE THAN IT WAS 20 YEARS AGO?

I DON'T THINK IT IS TOO DIFFERENT. THE COMIC STRIP AND SARDONIC, LAZY CHARACTERS (MY FAVOURITE TYPE) HAVE BEEN AROUND SINCE PRINT. WE JUST SEE MORE OF A GLOBAL SPREAD NOW AND MORE PEOPLE PRODUCING GREAT GRAPHICS, GREAT COMMENTARY AND GREAT CHARACTERS. I GUESS IT IS EASY FOR ANYONE TO DO THIS AND SO THEN HAS BECOME MUCH MORE PROLIFIC.

WHAT IS THE MOST CHALLENGING ASPECT OF YOUR APPROACH? HOW DID YOU GET IT SORTED OUT?

CREATING GRAPHICS AND ILLUSTRATIONS FOR MY BRAND IS ALWAYS AN ENJOYABLE CHALLENGE. I GUESS FOR ME IT IS ALWAYS: HOW DO I KEEP IT FRESH BUT STILL MAKE IT RELATE BACK TO OUR BRAND LAZY OAF? I HAVE TO ALWAYS REMEMBER TO KEEP IT WITTY AND IRREVERENT. I MAKE A BIG EFFORT TO KEEP IT THIS WAY AND IT IS ALSO IMPORTANT FOR ME TO DO THIS WITH MY DUMB WAY OF DRAWING AND MY REFERENCE POINTS, WHICH ARE NEARLY ALWAYS PIZZA.

SOMETIMES YOU FORGET WHY YOU DO WHAT YOU DO AND WHY THE HELL PEOPLE BUY YOUR STUFF. IT IS ALWAYS NICE TO BE REMINDED THAT PEOPLE ACTUALLY LIKE IT BECAUSE WE ARE FUNNY, LOUD AND IRREVERENT.

YOU WORKED WITH SOME OF OUR BELOVED CHILDHOOD CHARACTERS IN THE LATEST COLLECTIONS SUCH AS GARFIELD AND LOONEY TUNES. HOW DID THE IDEAS COME INTO PLACE?

I ALWAYS DESIGN WITH TEENAGE NOSTALGIA IN MIND, AND CHARACTERS FROM WHEN I WAS A TEEN THAT ALWAYS APPEAR ON MY MOOD BOARDS. I KNEW I COULD DO SOMETHING FRESH WITH THESE CHARACTERS THAT NO ONE ELSE WAS CURRENTLY DOING. HOPEFULLY I MANAGED TO DO THAT. IT WASN'T JUST ABOUT LICENSING A CHARACTER. I LIKE TO DO PROJECTS THAT ARE PERSONAL AND I HAVE AFFECTION FOR ALL OF THESE CHARACTERS.

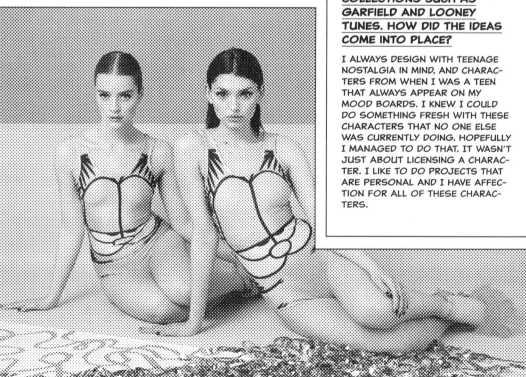

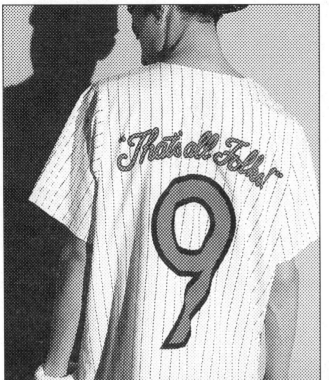

SO FOR SUMMER 2015 THE GIRL I WAS DESIGNING FOR WAS A BIG DORK. SHE WEARS BIG OL' GLASSES THAT AREN'T FASHIONABLE. HER INTERESTS INCLUDE ANCIENT EGYPT, SCIENCE FICTION AND ANIME. SHE PROBABLY HAS A RABBIT AND LIKES PAINTING WATERCOLOUR PORTRAITS OF SMALL MAMMALS.

CARTOON GRAPHICS ARE NO STRANGER TO THE FASHION SCENE. HOW DOES LAZY OAF CATCH THE EYE AMIDST SUCH TREND?

LAZY OAF USES PRINTS IN A VERY CONFIDENT WAY. WE DON'T DO SMALL AND SIMPLE. WE GO BIG AND LOUD SO HOPEFULLY THAT GETS YOUR ATTENTION!

WHY DO YOUR OFTEN TAKE REFERENCE FROM FOOD, ESPECIALLY FAST FOOD, IN YOUR DESIGN?

FAST FOOD IS THE ULTIMATE LAZY FOOD. I THINK IT GOES WITH THE BRAND AND I TOTALLY LOVE IT. IT IS ALSO SYNONYMOUS WITH TEENAGE CULTURE AND LAZY LIVING. I DON'T GET THE FUSS ABOUT SALAD!

DO YOU ACTUALLY DEVELOP A STORYLINE FOR THE CHARACTERS AND OBJECTS YOU CREATE? CAN YOU SHARE WITH US ONE STORY YOU LOVE MOST?

SOMETIMES I DO, I LIKE TO CREATE A MUSE FOR EACH COLLECTION SO I CAN UNDERSTAND THE LOOK AND FEEL OF THE CHARACTER AND IMAGINE WHAT SHE WOULD WEAR.

WHAT IS YOUR FAVOURITE GRAPHIC NOVEL OR ANIMATED CARTOON? WHY IS IT SPECIAL TO YOU?

I LOVE "THE SIMPSONS", "FUTURAMA" (CLASSICS); I ALSO LOVE GARFIELD GROWING UP AND READ ALL THE STRIPS IN BOOK FORMATS. GARFIELD WAS SUCH A GREAT CHARACTER, SIMILAR TO HOMER IN A WAY. HE WAS LAZY, QUICK WITTED AND FOOD OBSESSED.

IF YOU ARE TO APPLY YOUR WORK ONTO OTHER ARTEFACTS, WHAT WOULD IT BE?

I WOULD LOVE TO DO A CAR PROJECT, A HOUSE OR A CAFÉ. I HAVE RECENTLY GOT A DOG AND AM VERY FRUSTRATED AT THE LACK OF COOL DOG PRODUCTS, SO MAYBE THAT.

WHAT ARE YOU PLANNING ON DOING NEXT? IS THERE SOMETHING YOU'RE EAGER TO EXPLORE?

I HAVE LOADS OF PLANS AND TOO MUCH WORK! WE ARE GOING TO DO A FEW SPECIAL COLLABORATIONS, WHICH ARE EXCITING. AT THE MOMENT I AM GEARING UP TO DESIGN THE NEXT COLLECTION AW15 AND THINKING ABOUT CHRISTMAS!

I WOULD LOVE TO DO MORE COLLABORATIVE PROJECTS AS IN PRODUCT PROJECTS. I LOVED COLLABORATING WITH SHOE BRANDS AS IT ALWAYS PROVIDES NEW AND INTERESTING CHALLENGES AND I LIKE TO BE CHEEKY AND SEE HOW FAR WE CAN GO WITH IT! MAYBE A CAR PROJECT?

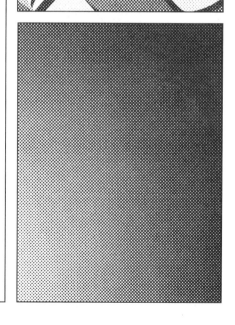

DIALOGUE WITH...

MARTÍN VITALITI!

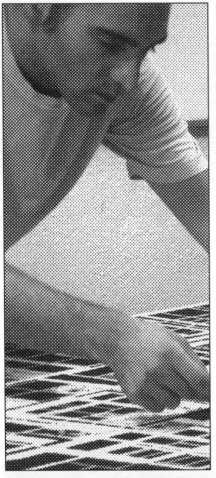

WHAT DO YOU LOVE ABOUT COMICS? WHY DO YOU THINK IT IS EFFECTIVE TO GET THE IDEAS ACROSS THROUGH THIS MEDIUM?

THE COMMUNICATION SYSTEM OF COMICS IS MERGED BY TWO KINDS OF ART: DRAWING (IN THE BROADEST INTERPRETATION OF THE WORD) AND LITERATURE. A SORT OF DIAGRAM COMBINES THE NARRATIVE AND THE IMAGES. SIGNIFICANT IMAGES ARE MEANT TO BE READ, AND WRITTEN WORDS, WITH GREAT TYPOGRAPHICAL CREATIVITY, ARE MEANT TO BE LOOKED AT. SILENTLY, COMICS EXHIBIT THE ENGINEERING OF THE ELEMENTS THAT MAKE VISIBLE WHAT IS INVISIBLE, LIKE THE SOUND OR THE VOICES. IT IS A STATIC FORMAT THAT REPRESENTS THE PASSING OF TIME — WITHOUT ANY TRICKS OR ANYTHING TO HIDE — ON THE SURFACE OF THE PAGE. BECAUSE OF THE MEDIUM'S ECONOMY, MATERIALLY CONSTRUCTED BY INK AND PAPER, COMICS CONTAIN ENOUGH POTENTIAL TO SIGNIFICANTLY BLOW UP AN IDEA AND EXPAND IT MASSIVELY THROUGH ITS PUBLICATION.

PROFILE

Particularly drawn to the inconspicuous details of comics, Martín Vitaliti has developed a line of work in which he reworks and creates new meaning from the deposition and narrative of the Pop Art form by disintegration, repetition, collage and isolation. Born in Buenos Aires and currently based in Barcelona, Vitaliti has collated his unique views on the language of comics and published a trilogy namely Líneas cinéticas (2008), Didascalias (2012) and Fondos (2012). Vitaliti is a resident artist at HANGAR, Barcelona as of 2014.

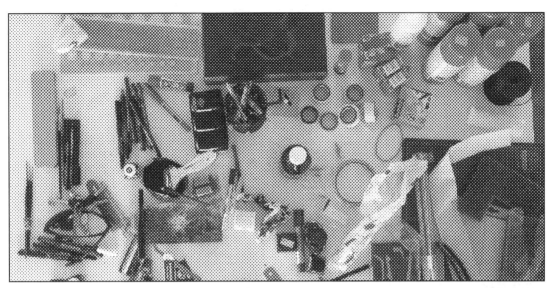

HOW DIFFERENT IN YOUR OPINION IS TODAY'S PORTRAYAL OF POP CULTURE THAN IT WAS 20 YEARS AGO?

COMIC STRIPS HAVE FOR LONG BEEN CONSIDERED A MINOR ART FORM. ITS ORIGIN LIES WITHIN THE ENTERTAINMENT INDUSTRY, PART OF THE PUBLISHING BUSINESS. A POSITION THAT WEAKENED THE ARTISTIC POSSIBILITIES OF ITS LANGUAGE AND DESTINED IT TO BE THE 'YOUNGER SIBLING' OF THE ARTS. IN THIS HISTORICAL CONTEXT THERE WERE ALWAYS AUTHORS WHO WOULD SKILFULLY GENERATE ROOM FOR OTHER KINDS OF DISCOURSE, LIKE THE COMPLEX AND PSYCHOLOGICAL ASPECTS OF THE CHARACTERS OR RECOGNISING POLITICAL AND SOCIAL DIFFERENCES. THIS ARTISTIC INDIVIDUALITY THAT TODAY CAN BE CHALLENGED OR JUDGED ON THE SAME LEVEL AS OTHER ARTS LIKE LITERATURE OR CINEMA, ETC.

WHAT IS THE MOST CHALLENGING ASPECT OF YOUR APPROACH?

IN ORDER TO MAKE COMICS, ONE MUST APPLY TO CERTAIN STRICT RULES AND LIVE BY THEM. SOMEHOW MY WORK IS IN RESPONSE TO THESE CONSTRICTIONS. I SUPPOSE I INTENT TO BEND THE RULES THROUGH A DIALOGUE WITH THE MEDIUM. THE ARTISTIC DIFFICULTIES THAT MIGHT EMERGE FROM THIS TASK ARE PROBABLY THE SAME AS WHAT AN AUTHOR OF COMICS MUST DEAL WITH WHEN CHOOSING WHAT TO EXPLAIN AND HOW TO DO IT.

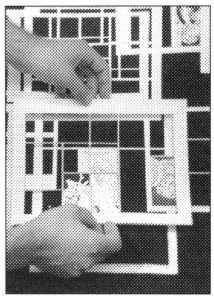

WHAT IS YOUR FAVOURITE GRAPHIC NOVEL OR ANIMATED CARTOON? WHY IS IT SPECIAL TO YOU?

DEPENDING ON THE MOMENT I FIND MYSELF IN, I COULD NAME ONE OR ANOTHER. MY FAVOURITE WORKS ARE BY THOSE AUTHORS WHOM APPROACH THE MEDIUM IN A VISIONARY WAY, WHO LOOK FOR OTHER STYLISTIC FORMS BY MEANS OF BOTH IMAGES AND IN THE RHETORICAL ASPECTS, AND GENERATE A TWIST OR TENSION TOWARDS A DISCOURSE THAT CAN GENERATE KNOWLEDGE.

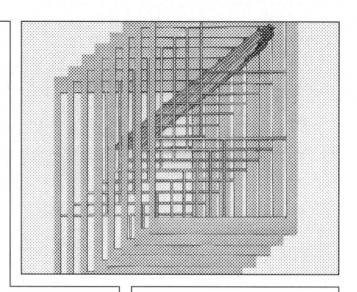

COMIC GRIDS ARE INTEGRAL TO YOUR CREATION. IN WHAT WAY DO THESE GRIDS APPEAL TO YOU?

THE USE OF GRID AS AN ELEMENT ORIGINATES IN ITS SIGNIFICANT PRESENCE IN THE COMICS' ORGANISATIONAL SYSTEM. MY INTENTION IS TO MAKE THIS SYSTEM EVIDENT AND AMPLIFY ITS MEANING IN 'REAL LIFE'. IN SOME WORKS THE GRID TAKES ON ONE MORPHOLOGY AND IN OTHERS ANOTHER. BASICALLY IT JUST SYMBOLISES AN EVER-CHANGING STRUCTURE THAT SUSTAINS AND ORGANISES US.

YOUR WORK OFTEN CREATES DIMENSIONS BY BREAKING FRAMES AND PAGES. WHAT'S YOUR CONCEPT BEHIND?

IN THESE CASES MY MOTIVATION IS TO WORK WITH THE LIMITS OF THE FORMAT, THE MEDIUM. DELIBERATELY DECONSTRUCTING IT MAKES THIS CONSTRICTION EVIDENT AND ALSO OPENS A SPATIAL DIMENSION. I MEAN TO LET WHATEVER ACTION HAPPEN WITHIN THE FRAME (REPRESENTATIONALLY) AND EXPAND (BY BEING PRESENTED) PHYSICALLY

OUTSIDE ITS ORIGINAL SPACE — THE COMIC BOOK — IN ORDER TO INHABIT OUR SPACE.

CAN YOU TELL US SOMETHING ABOUT YOUR CREATIVE PROCESS? ARE THESE ORIGINAL COMIC STRIPS THAT YOU USE? WHERE DID YOU SOURCE THEM?

THERE ARE TWO WAYS FOR IT TO BEGIN: FROM A PREVIOUS IDEA, I SEARCH FOR AN APPROPRIATE SITUATION WITHIN THE MEDIUM IN ORDER TO MAKE THE WORK HAPPEN; OR THE UNSUSPECTED DISCOVERY WHILE READING OR RESEARCHING PUBLICATIONS. ONCE THE SITUATION IS LOCATED, I THINK ABOUT HOW TO RECONSTRUCT IT, ISOLATING CERTAIN ESSENTIAL ELEMENTS, COMBINING AND UNITING THEM TO MODIFY THE NARRATIVE EFFECTS. I SEEK TO STRENGTHEN THE ALREADY EXISTING INTENTION OF THE CHOSEN SITUATION, AS WELL AS TO REINFORCE IT NARRATIVELY IN THE OPPOSITE DIRECTION. I USE APPROPRIATION, INTERVENTION, COLLAGE, DRAWING OR INSTALLATION.

MOST OF MY WORKS EMERGE FROM 'ORIGINAL' MAGAZINES, OFTEN REPEATED IN THE SAME PIECE. I INTERVENE THE COPIES — BECAUSE A COMIC MAGAZINE IS NOTHING MORE

THAN A *COPY* OF ANOTHER *ORIGINAL* — AND THE RESULT ACQUIRES THE MATERIAL VALUE OF AN ORIGINAL. THE FACT THAT I WORK WITH PUBLISHED COMIC BOOKS FROM DIFFERENT PERIODS SUPPOSES AN ARCHAEOLOGICAL ACTIVITY WHERE THE SEARCH OF THIS 'APPROPRIATE SITUATION' IS USUALLY MUCH MORE TIME-CONSUMING THAN THE ACTUAL EXECUTION OF THE WORK.

YOU TAKE GRAPHICAL REFERENCE MOSTLY FROM AMERICAN COMICS. DO YOU READ ASIAN COMICS TOO? WHAT DO YOU THINK OF THEM?

IT IS NOT PARTICULARLY LIKE I AM A FOLLOWER OF THE GENRE OF SUPERHEROES. BUT IT IS TRUE THAT I FIND A SPECIAL LEVEL OF DRAWING AND TEXTUAL TOPICS AND DYNAMICS IN THESE PUBLICATIONS THAT ALLOW ME TO DEVELOP A CERTAIN LINE OF WORK. I ALSO TAKE REFERENCE FROM A LOT OF OTHER COMICS BY AUTHORS FROM PLACES OTHER THAN THE STATES. MY APPROACH IS BASED ON COMICS IN GENERAL, WHATEVER THE ORIGIN. I ATTEMPT TO REINFORCE THE ESSENCE OF EACH AND EVERY ONE OF THEM, THEIR DISPOSITION AND THEIR NARRATIVE. THIS WAY THE TYPE OF COMICS OR STYLE I APPROPRIATE IS AS CLOSE AS POSSIBLE TO THE IDEA I AM DEVELOPING, BUT WITHOUT TAKING IT AWAY FROM ITS OWN CHARACTER.

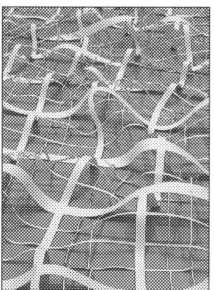

WHAT IS THE MOST INTERESTING FEEDBACK YOU HAVE GOT SO FAR ABOUT YOUR WORK?

WHAT FILLS ME WITH SATISFACTION IS WHEN I MEET PEOPLE WITH AN INTEREST AND KNOWLEDGE OF COMICS WHO RECOGNISE AND APPRECIATE MY WORK THE SAME WAY IT IS APPRECIATED FROM WITHIN THE ART WORLD.

WHAT ARE YOU PLANNING ON DOING NEXT? IS THERE SOMETHING YOU'RE EAGER TO EXPLORE?

THE PLAN IS ALWAYS TO WORK IN MY STUDIO. IT IS THE ONLY MOMENT AND PLACE WHERE THINGS CAN EMERGE OR HAPPEN WHEN IT COMES TO WORKS LIKE MINE. I HAVE A LOT OF MATERIAL YET TO EXPLORE. WHAT WILL HAPPEN IS UNPREDICTABLE. BUT I AM ALWAYS EAGER TO FIND OUT.

DIALOGUE WITH...

PHILIP COLBERT!

PROFILE

A concept rather than a fashion label created and led by British artist and designer Philip Colbert, The Rodnik Band presents a bold, fun, Pop Art-inspired view of haute couture and a lavish take on ready-to-wear. Mixing fashion with influences of music and art, Colbert dares people to walk in Van Gogh's sunflowers, Marcel Duchamp's urinal and Andy Warhol's Campbell's soup can and make clothing a thoughtful statement with unorthodox tailoring and handmade prints. The music elements come as songs which Colbert writes for each collection and performs at respective fashion shows.

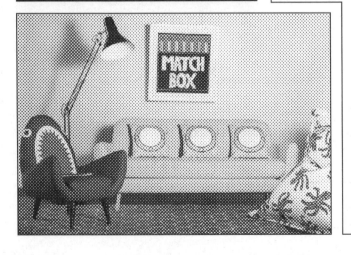

WHAT DO YOU LOVE ABOUT POP ART? WHY DO YOU THINK IT IS EFFECTIVE TO GET YOUR IDEAS ACROSS THROUGH THIS MEDIUM?

I THINK OF MYSELF AS A POP ARTIST WHO MAKES CLOTHES! FOR ME POP ART IS THE MOST DIRECT FORM OF COMMUNICATION. IT IS THE MOST DEMOCRATIC AND ACCESSIBLE ART FORM! I LOVE HOW DIRECT, HUMOROUS AND SHOCKING IT CAN BE! HUMOUR HELPS TO SHAKE THE CAGE OF OUR LIMITED UNDERSTANDING YET MAKE THINGS FUN AT THE SAME TIME! ART CAN OFTEN TAKE ITSELF TOO SERIOUSLY AND GET LOST IN ITS OWN ILLUSIONS OF GRANDEUR AND REALISE THAT NOTHING'S REALLY THERE! FOR CLOTHING, POP ART WORKS BECAUSE IT LITERALLY MAKES AN OUTFIT POP AND COMMUNICATE DIRECTLY, AS FASHION, TOO, OFTEN GETS LOST IN AMBIGUOUS MEANING AND TREND OVER SUBSTANCE. I LIKE IDEAS THAT COMMUNICATE TO EVERYONE, AND GIVE PEOPLE A CHANCE TO RELAX AND ESCAPE FROM THE SHACKLES OF REALITY!

SEQUINS" DRESSES ARE VERY LABOUR-INTENSIVE TOO, AS THEY ARE ALL HAND-STITCHED. I LIKE THE IDEA THAT THESE DRESSES ARE A WORK OF ART ALSO IN THE SENSE OF THEIR CRAFTSMANSHIP.

PEANUTS, ONE OF THE WORLD'S MOST BELOVED CHILDHOOD CHARACTERS, PREVAILS ANOTHER COLLECTION. HOW DID THE IDEAS COME INTO PLACE?

THEY APPROACHED ME! AND I THOUGHT IT WAS A PERFECT FIT! FOR ME THE PARTNERSHIP IS A FUN CREATIVE MIX OF THE WORLDS, I LIKE TO THINK OF IT LIKE THE PEANUTS CHARACTERS ARE MY PALS, AND THEY ARE HANGING OUT IN THE RODNIK WORLD.

"VENUS IN SEQUINS" IS AN HOMAGE TO THE WORK OF MARCEL DUCHAMP, ANDY WARHOL AND VAN GOGH. WHAT DO THESE ARTISTS MEAN TO YOU? WHAT IS THE NOTION BEHIND MAKING ART WEARABLE?

THESE ARE GREAT ARTISTS. THEIR WORK HAS LAID THE FOUNDATIONS OF IDEAS THAT OTHER ARTISTS TODAY NOW STAND ON! I LIKE THE IDEA OF RECYCLING THESE ICONS OF ART INTO SOMETHING WITH A NEW DIMENSION. TO MAKE AN ARTWORK WEARABLE CHANGES ITS NATURE AND GIVES IT A NEW LEASE OF LIFE. I LOVE THE IDEA OF CREATING A NEW GENRE OF WEARABLE ART! A CROSSOVER BETWEEN ART AND FASHION. AND TO CREATE THAT CONCEPT USING ICONS OF ART INTO WEARABLE DRESSES MADE THE PARODY AND TENSION MORE CLEAR. FOR ME CREATIVITY IS MIXING GENRES TO CREATE NEW CREATIVE GROUND, TAKING A STEP IN AN UNCHARTED TERRITORY.

THIS COLLECTION IS HANDMADE AND LIMITED TO AN EDITION OF FIVE. WILL YOU REFER TO IT AS AN 'HAUTE COUTURE COLLECTION'?

HAUTE COUTURE IS THE PART OF FASHION WHICH IS MOST LIKE ARTWORK! IT'S LIMITED IN SUPPLY, UNIQUE AND EXCLUSIVE AND VERY LABOUR INTENSIVE. THE "VENUS IN

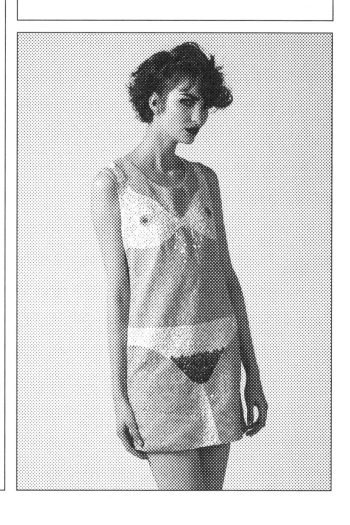

WHAT IS THE MOST CHALLENGING ASPECT OF YOUR APPROACH? HOW DID YOU GET IT SORTED OUT?

THE BUSINESS SIDE OF FASHION IS TRICKY, SO I HAVE LEARNED TO WORK IN MY OWN PACE AND DO THINGS ON MY OWN TERMS, OTHERWISE THE HAMSTER WHEEL OF FASHION CAN EXHAUST AND DILUTE YOU.

SENSE OF HUMOUR SEEMS TO GUIDE THROUGH THE RODNIK BAND'S CREATIONS. WHAT IN ESSENCE DO YOU WISH TO CONVEY IN YOUR COLLECTIONS? HOW DO YOU CHOOSE YOUR THEMES?

YES I BELIEVE THE RODNIK DESIGNS HAVE A POSITIVE FUN ENERGY THAT CAN BE A CATALYST FOR POSITIVE THINGS TO HAPPEN. OFTEN IDEAS SORT OF DISTIL IN MY MIND. I MIGHT SEE A GRAPHIC OF PASTA TUBES WHILE COOKING AND FEEL THERE IS SOMETHING ICONIC AND INTERESTING ABOUT IT. AND THE IMAGE MIGHT STAY IN MY MIND. FOR ME, THE INTERESTING IDEAS ARE THE ONES THAT STAY IN YOUR MIND OVER TIME, THAT HAVE HAD A SUBTLE IMPACT. I LIKE TO THEN PUT THIS FORWARD IN MY VISUAL STYLE.

YOU HAVE A BACKGROUND IN PHILOSOPHY RATHER THAN FASHION DESIGN. HOW DID YOU GET INTO THE INDUSTRY? WHAT'S YOUR PHILOSOPHY OF FASHION AND DESIGN?

I LIKE TO THINK THAT I HAVE A PHILOSOPHICAL APPROACH TO DESIGN. FOR ME THE ETHOS AND PHILOSOPHY OF THE CLOTHES ARE WHAT I AM ACTUALLY SELLING. MY PHILOSOPHY IS THAT OF A POSITIVE SARCASTIC ONE. I BELIEVE THE GREATEST FORM OF UNDERSTANDING IS THROUGH HUMOUR. TO PLAYFULLY SHAKE THE CAGE IS THE CLOSEST WE GET TO TRUTH. I ALSO BELIEVE IN THE POWER OF A POSITIVE PLAYFUL ATTITUDE. I BELIEVE IT CAN BE A CATALYST FOR ENERGY THAT CAN MAKE DREAMS COME TRUE!

HOW DIFFERENT IN YOUR OPINION IS TODAY'S PORTRAYAL OF POP CULTURE THAN IT WAS 20 YEARS AGO?

THE CHALLENGE OF POP IS KEEPING IT FRESH AND RELEVANT AS 80S POP IS OFTEN OVERUSED, ETC. I STILL LOVE IT! BUT I AM AWARE OF THE NEED TO PUSH POP FORWARD AS I STILL BELIEVE IN THE POWER OF POP! LIKE ANYTHING IT JUST NEEDS A REFRESH AND NEW IDEAS!!

WHAT IS YOUR FAVOURITE GRAPHIC NOVEL OR ANIMATED CARTOON? WHAT IS IT SPECIAL TO YOU?

I LOVE TINTIN! IT'S ALL ABOUT CHARMING ADVENTURES WHAT'S NOT TO LOVE?!

WHAT ARE YOU PLANNING ON DOING NEXT? IS THERE SOMETHING YOU'RE EAGER TO EXPLORE?

I AM WORKING ON MY FIRST ART SHOW, OF LARGE SEQUIN ON CANVAS PAINTINGS. BRINGING MY POP WORLD INTO THE GALLERY FOR SOME FUN! ALSO WE RECENTLY LAUNCHED RODNIK INTERIORS WITH MADE.COM, POP ART INTERIORS WHICH HAS BEEN GREAT FUN, AND AM KEEN TO KEEP DEVELOPING THIS.

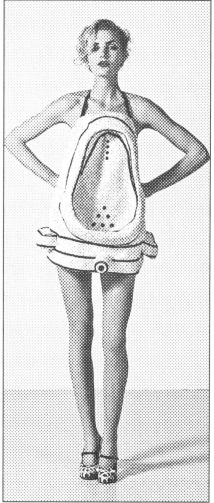

DIALOGUE WITH...

PROFILE

Born in Hong Kong and trained as a graphic artist in the UK, Rex Koo mixes cultural influences in his work. This is particularly visible in his typographic art and the subjects of his recent illustration project "Simple People", which he initiated as a personal venture in 2012. Within the collection, all characters were conceived with angular forms, created based on grids, the most basic element in graphic design. For Koo, drawing is simply perpetually a realm where he can constantly explore and confront himself.

WHAT DOES POP CULTURE MEAN TO YOU?

I THINK THE MEANING OF POP CULTURE VARIES WITH TIME. BECAUSE THE MEDIA HAS EVOLVED AND TECHNOLOGY MADE CONSIDERABLE STRIDES, WHAT WE REFER TO AS POPULAR CULTURE TODAY IS COMPLETELY DIFFERENT FROM WHAT IT WAS IN THE 60S AND 70S. IT CAN BE TIRESOME OR EXCITING, COMPREHENSIBLE OR CONFUSING. IT IS THIS DIVERSITY AND DISPARITY THAT HAS BEEN KEEPING UP MY CLOSE INTEREST IN THE POP CULTURE AROUND THE WORLD.

WHAT DO YOU DRAW IN GENERAL?

BASICALLY ANYTHING CAN BE MY SUBJECT, BUT STILL I'M MOST ATTRACTED TO HUMAN FACES. SO, PORTRAITS MAKE UP MOST OF MY WORK.

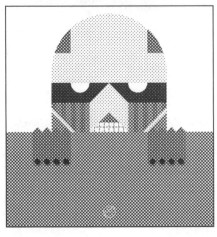

WHY DID YOU WISH TO EXPAND YOUR GRAPHIC DESIGN SKILLS TO PAINTING AND ILLUSTRATION IN THE FIRST PLACE? HOW EFFECTIVE IS IT TO GET YOUR IDEAS ACROSS THROUGH GRAPHIC ILLUSTRATIONS?

THE KEY DIFFERENCE BETWEEN GRAPHIC DESIGN AND IL-LUSTRATION IS THAT ILLUSTRATION CAN BE MADE AS ONE PLEASES. IT COULD BE A MEANS OF EXPRESSION, AN EMO-TIONAL OUTLET, OR SIMPLY ILLUSTRATION. ON THE CON-TRARY, GRAPHIC DESIGN IS MADE FOR A PURPOSE. IT CAR-RIES FUNCTIONS SPECIFICALLY DEVISED FOR A PROJECT OR A THEME, AND IS THEREFORE COMMERCIAL BY NATURE. YOU CAN'T DESIGN GRAPHICS JUST FOR GRAPHICS' SAKE. IN OTHER WORDS, I WILL NOT BE ABLE TO CREATE GRAPHICS SIMPLY TO EXPRESS MY FEELINGS WITHOUT A CLIENT.

BECAUSE I HAVE DEVELOPED A CAREER AS A GRAPHIC DESIGNER AND BEEN DRAWING AT THE SAME TIME, ONE DAY I THOUGHT ABOUT HOW IT WOULD LOOK IF I APPLY GRAPHIC DESIGN SKILLS (E.G. THE USE OF SUBTLE GRAPHIC SYMBOLS) TO PORTRAIT ILLUSTRATIONS. THAT'S HOW SIM-PLE PEOPLE CAME TO LIVE.

YOU HAVE BEEN ADOPTING A GRID BASE TO ILLUSTRATE. WHY GRIDS? WHAT'S THE FUN ABOUT SIMPLIFYING POPULAR CHARACTERS INTO SHAPES?

SINCE THE IDEA OF 'SIMPLE' IS CORE TO "SIMPLE PEOPLE", I HAVE TO PLACE A LIMIT ON THE COMPOSITION'S COM-PLEXITY. GRID IS INSTRUMENTAL IN ACHIEVING THIS QUALITY,

AND MAINTAINING COHERENCE OF THE COLLECTION AT ONCE, THOUGH IT ALSO RESTRICTS THE WAY I DRAW, ESPECIALLY THE CURVES, WHICH CONSTANTLY CHALLENGES ME TO COME UP WITH NEW WAYS TO PRESENT IDEAS. THIS IS EXACTLY WHAT MAKES CREATING "SIMPLE PEOPLE" SO INTERESTING — LIMITATIONS HAVE INSPIRED UNLIM-ITEDNESS.

"SIMPLE PEOPLE" CONTAINS CARTOON ICONS FROM THE WESTERN CULTURE, JAPAN AND HONG KONG. HOW DO YOU FIND THEM DIFFERENT IN TERMS OF CHARACTER AND STYLE?

I PRINCIPALLY CHOSE MY SUBJECTS BASED ON TWO THINGS. FIRST, IT HAS TO BE MY FAVOURITE CHAR-ACTER. SECOND, IT GOT TO HAVE A STRONG PERSONALITY, BE IN-STANTLY RECOGNISABLE FOR THE WAY IT DRESSES AND LOOKS, OR BE KNOWN FOR GREAT ACHIEVEMENTS. FOR ME, WHAT THEY SHARE IN COM-MON IS THAT THEY CAN BE EASILY CONDENSED INTO SIMPLE GRAPHICS.

HOW MUCH DOES "SIMPLE PEOPLE" SAY ABOUT YOU? DO YOU CONSIDER IT A PERSONAL PROJECT?

"SIMPLE PEOPLE" IS INCREDIBLY SIGNIFICANT TO ME. IT IS LIKE A SUMMATION OF MY PHILOSOPHY OF AND MY OUTLOOK ON LIFE, AND MY 15-YEAR CAREER IN GRAPHIC DESIGN. IT IS MY ANSWER TO "WHAT'S CREATIVE WORK?" IT IS, BY FAR, MOST PRECISELY, THE VERY EMBODIMENT OF MY CREATIVE STYLE. NOT ONLY IS IT A PERSONAL WORK, BUT ALSO THE ACTUALISATION OF MY THOUGHTS AND PHILOSOPHIES.

HOW WOULD YOU DESCRIBE HONG KONG'S COMIC SCENE? WHICH CHARACTER WOULD YOU SAY IS MOST REPRESENTATIVE OF HONG KONG AND WHY?

CREATIVITY HAS BEEN STRIKINGLY ABSENT FROM HONG KONG'S CLASSICS. CONVERSELY, READING THE RECENT WAVE OF GRAPHIC NOVELS THAT HAS DISPLAYED A RATHER ALTERNATIVE APPROACH TO COMICS AND GREATER RESONANCES FOR YOUNG READERS WILL MAKE FOR A MORE ENRICHING EXPERIENCE. I THINK THE MOST SERIOUS SHORTCOMING OF HONG KONG'S COMICS, MOVIES AND TV DRAMAS IS THE SHORT OF INTERESTING TOPICS, CONTENT, AND DISTINCTIVE PLOTS.

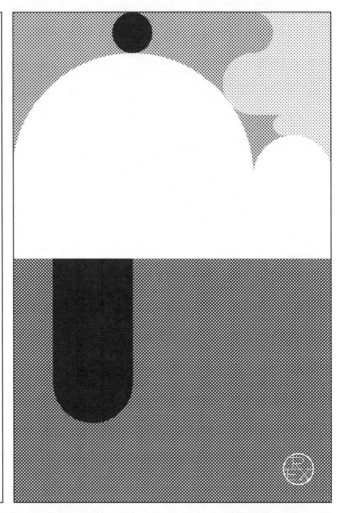

ONLY RARELY ONE CAN SPORT A WELL-DESIGNED NARRATIVE STRUCTURE IN THESE PUBLICATIONS, PROGRAMMES AND FILMS.

IF I AM TO CHOOSE AN ARCHETYPE OF HONGKONGERS FROM HOMEGROWN COMICS, IT WOULD DEFINITELY BE MASTER Q, WHO ALSO APPEARED IN MY "SIMPLE PEOPLE" COLLECTION, BECAUSE OF ITS MULTIPLICITY. HE COULD BE A RICH MAN AND A TRAMP, A BOXER ONE MINUTE AND A MONK THE NEXT. HE IS A GRAPHIC PORTRAYAL OF THE PLURALISTIC SOCIETY OF HONG KONG.

WHAT ARE YOUR FAVOURITE COMICS OR CARTOONS TO DATE? WHY ARE THEY SPECIAL TO YOU?

"PHOENIX" BY OSAMU TEZUKA. THE SERIES HAS NOT ONLY DISPLAYED MAGNIFICENT VISION AND WORLD VIEWS WITHIN THE CONTEXT OF LIFE, DEATH, AND THE CYCLE OF REBIRTH, BUT ALSO FAIRLY REVOLUTIONARY CONCEPTS OF 'TIME' CONSIDERING THE TIME IT WAS COMPOSED. THE MANGA IS OF SUCH PROFOUND INSIGHT THAT BEWILDERS AND TOUCHES ME.

WHAT ARE YOU PLANNING ON DOING NEXT? IS THERE SOMETHING YOU'RE EAGER TO EXPLORE?

IN THE PAST SIX MONTHS, "SIMPLE PEOPLE" HAS BEEN COLLABORATING WITH A RANGE OF BRANDS TO LAUNCH PRODUCTS SUCH AS PRINT TEES, IPHONE CASES, AND MUGS. APART FROM THAT I WOULD ALSO HOPE TO EXPLORE MORE POSSIBILITIES, IDEALLY SOMETHING OTHER THAN CONSUMER GOODS. OTHER THAN THIS, I AM ALSO PREPARING TO PUBLISH AN ILLUSTRATION BOOK ABOUT HONG KONG FILMS. I ALREADY STARTED WORKING ON THESE ILLUSTRATIONS TWO YEARS AGO, BUT STILL CANNOT DETERMINE HOW THEY SHOULD BE PUBLISHED.

IF YOU WERE TO BECOME A SUPERHERO, WHAT SUPERPOWER DO YOU POSSESS?

THERE SEEMS TO BE A CHARACTER IN "X-MEN" WHO CAN TELEPORT ACROSS SPACE. I THINK THIS CAPTIVATES ME MOST, SINCE SUCH POWER WOULD ALLOW ME TO HAVE TEA SNACKS IN PARIS, AMBLE IN KYOTO, WATCH THE SUN SET AT THE TIP OF A PYRAMID, AND EVERYTHING ELSE I WANT AT ANYTIME I WISH. THE MOST CRITICAL ADVANTAGE IS THAT THIS COULD ESSENTIALLY OBVIATE THE PAINFUL PLANE TRIPS TO AND FROM THESE DESTINATIONS.

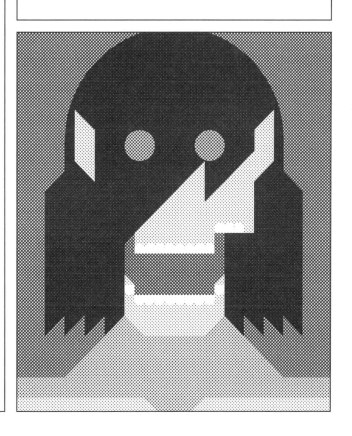

DIALOGUE WITH... SANDRA CHEVRIER!

PROFILE

A gaze collector, an idea chaser and a single mom, Sandra Chevrier uses collage or the loose and heavy texture of paint that make the women of her art emerge from their world within the canvas, like a dance between reality and imagination, truth and deception. In salute to women's willpower and strength to overcome the hurdles in life, Chevrier's illustrations expose the limitations within our world, our self-imposed expectations and the cages we have allowed to bar us from fullness of life's experience.

WHAT DO YOU LOVE ABOUT COMICS? WHY DO YOU THINK IT IS EFFECTIVE TO GET THE IDEAS ACROSS THROUGH THIS MEDIUM?

PEOPLE TEND TO DRAW CLOSER TO WHAT IS FAMILIAR TO THEM ALREADY. THOSE WHO COME ACROSS MY WORK AND FIND AN IMAGE OF SUPERMAN ARE MORE LIKELY TO STOP FOR A GAZE OWING TO THE FACT THAT IT'S ALREADY ESTABLISHED POPULARITY. IT IS AFTER THIS INITIAL CONTACT THAT THE VIEWER CAN REACH DEEPER TO THE SIGNIFICANCE OF THE WORK, THE TRUE MESSAGE.

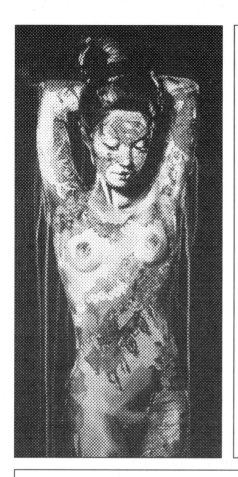

YOU ARE A 'GAZE COLLECTOR'. WHAT KIND OF GAZES DO YOU COLLECT?

I NEED TO FEEL THAT THERE IS A STORY HIDING BENEATH THE EYES. EYES ARE THE MIRROR OF THE SOUL, SOMETIMES YOU LOOK INTO THE EYES OF SOMEONE AND YOU CAN UNDERSTAND WHERE HE OR SHE COMES FROM. I WORK WITH EYES THAT SPEAK TO THE SPECTATOR, THAT CREATE AN ATTRACTION OR CHANNEL EMOTIONS.

WHAT ARE THE STORIES BEHIND THE GIRLS YOU PORTRAY? IS THERE ANY COMMON TRAITS AMONG THEM?

THE COMMON TRAITS WOULD BE THE EMOTION I FIND IN THEIR GAZE OR THE FRAGILITY OR EXPRESSION OF THEIR FIGURES. I AM REALLY PICKY REGARDING THE CHOICES OF MODELS BUT WHEN I FIND ONE THAT I LOVE TO WORK WITH, THEY BECOME MY MUSE.

YOU OFTEN MASK AND DRESS GIRLS IN HEROIC COMICS. WHAT DO THEY SAY?

YES, THAT OFTEN IS AN UNDERSTATEMENT. IT HAS BECOME WHAT I DO EXCLUSIVELY. THE SERIES "CAGES" IS ABOUT WOMEN TRYING TO FIND FREEDOM FROM THE TWISTED PRECONCEPTIONS OF WHAT A WOMAN SHOULD OR SHOULDN'T BE IN THE SOCIETY. THESE WOMEN ENCASED IN THESE CAGES OF BRASH IMPOSING PAINT OR COMIC BOOKS THAT MASK THEIR VERY PERSON SYMBOLISE THE STRUGGLE THAT WOMEN GO THROUGH AMIDST THESE FALSE EXPECTATIONS OF BEAUTY AND PER-

FECTION AS WELL AS THE LIMITATIONS SOCIETY PLACES ON WOMEN, CORRUPTING WHAT TRULY IS BEAUTIFUL BY PLACING WOMEN IN THESE PRISONS OF IDENTITY. BY DOING SO, THE SOCIETY IS ASKING THEM TO BECOME SUPERHEROES.

WATERCOLOUR IS ALSO A KEY ELEMENT IN YOUR WORK. CAN YOU TELL US MORE ABOUT YOUR PREFERENCE TOWARD THIS MEDIUM?

I HAVE ONLY BEEN WORKING WITH WATERCOLOUR FOR THE PAST 2-3 YEARS. WHEN I STARTED TO MAKE ART I ONLY USED PENCIL, THEN AFTER A COUPLE OF YEARS I HAD TO START USING PAINT FOR UNIVERSITY SCHOOL PROJECTS. I REALLY DIDN'T LIKE IT AT FIRST. I WAS USING THE BRUSHES AS IF I WOULD BE USING A PENCIL BUT THEN I UNDERSTOOD THAT PAINT IS A MATERIAL AND YOU CAN PLAY WITH IT. THE WATERCOLOUR IS SUCH A NICE MEDIUM THAT YOU CAN CONTROL IT PARTIALLY BUT NOT TOTALLY SO YOU WILL ALWAYS HAVE SURPRISES IN THE END, AND THAT IS QUITE EXCITING. YOU LET THE WATER DANCE WITH THE COLOURS.

WHAT IS THE MOST CHALLENGING ASPECT OF YOUR APPROACH? HOW DID YOU GET IT SORTED OUT?

AGGRESSIVELY PURSUE A COMMON THREAD UNTIL IT IS WORN AWAY, NOT ALWAYS DOING THE SAME THING OVER AND OVER AGAIN, TRY TO MAKE A SERIES EVOLVE, AND TAKE SOME RISKS. AND WHEN IT'S DONE THEN YOU BEGIN ON A NEW PATH.

HOW DIFFERENT IN YOUR OPINION IS TODAY'S PORTRAYAL OF POP CULTURE THAN IT WAS 20 YEARS AGO?

ART IS A REPRESENTATION OF THE SOCIETY WE LIVE IN. THE MENTALITIES AND VALUES HAVE CHANGED AND WE ARE OP-PRESSED BY CONSUMPTION, INDUSTRIALISATION AND THE NEED OF PERFECTION AND AESTHETIC. THERE IS A NEED FOR ARTIST TO USE POP CULTURE. ART HAS A WAY TO TRY AND CHANGE MENTALITIES.

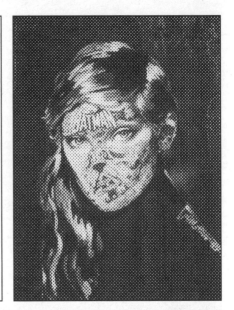

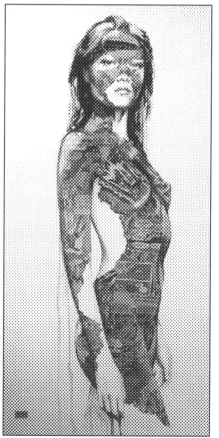

WHAT IS YOUR FAVOURITE GRAPHIC NOVEL OR ANIMATED CARTOON? WHAT IS IT SPECIAL TO YOU?

"THE DEATH OF SUPERMAN" AND THE BATMAN GRAPHIC NOVEL "A DEATH IN THE FAMILY". THEY BOTH PORTRAY A HUMAN SIDE OF THE SUPER-HUMAN CHARACTERS, A WEAKNESS, RENDERING THEM AS THOSE WHOM THE REST OF US CAN RELATE TO. SEEING SUPERMAN LAY HELPLESS IN LOIS LANE'S ARMS OR AN IMAGE OF BATMAN IN TEARS WHILE HIS PROTÉGÉ LAYS MOTIONLESS HAS AN INCREDIBLE IMPACT ON ME, GIVEN THE FEATS THAT THESE MEN ACCOMPLISH IN THEIR RESPECTIVE STORIES.

YOU TAKE GRAPHICAL REFERENCE MOSTLY FROM AMERICAN COMICS. DO YOU READ COMICS FROM OTHER PLACES TOO?

I HAVEN'T STEPPED OUT FURTHER FROM AMERICAN COMICS BECAUSE I AM USING IMAGES FROM COMICS THAT ARE ALREADY ESTABLISHED AND EASILY RECOGNISED AS SUPERHEROES SO AS TO STRESS THE SIGNIFICANCE OF MY WORK.

WHAT ARE YOU PLANNING ON DOING NEXT? IS THERE SOMETHING YOU'RE EAGER TO EXPLORE?

I WILL CONTINUE TO EXPLORE AND EXPERIMENT. I STILL HAVE A LOT OF IDEAS TO MAKE EVOLVE ABOUT THE SERIES "CAGES". I WILL KEEP THE METHOD BUT I WOULD LIKE TO FIND A WAY TO CHANGE THE MESSAGE BEHIND IT.

DIALOGUE WITH...
SIM CHANG!

PROFILE

Deriding himself as a 'homebody',
Taiwanese photographer Sim Chang
demonstrates profound thoughts and
understanding of his obsessive interests and Japanese cultural influences on Taiwan through his work.
Often sexually-charged, loaded with
scantily-clad girls and symbols
identified with young males' fanta-
sies, Chang's work speaks more of
ephemeral passions and love relationships, as well as politics and
social affairs, that should concern
the world. Here, Chang talks about
his views unreserved.

HOW DID YOU FALL IN LOVE WITH ANIME AND MANGA? HOW EFFECTIVE IT IS TO GET YOUR IDEAS ACROSS THROUGH THIS MEDIUM?

BY THE TIME I ATTENDED KINDERGARTEN, I READ MANGA
WITH MY ELDER BROTHER. THAT WAS HOW I LEARNED TO
WRITE. FOR ME, MANGA IS A PART OF MY LIFE. SOMETIMES
I FIND THE STORIES ODDLY FAMILIAR AND EMOTIONALLY
CONNECT WITH THEM. "COMIC BED", THE FIRST PIECE OF
"FLAWLESS LOVE", SHOULD SERVE AS AN EXAMPLE OF
HOW I CONSCIOUSLY PROJECTED MY STATE OF MIND INTO
SCENARIOS OF CARTOONS. "COMIC BED" WAS CREATED
AT A TIME WHEN I WAS ROMANTICALLY REJECTED, AND I
HAD LIKENED MY PSYCHOLOGICAL CONDITION TO THAT OF
A NURSE IN "NIGHT SHIFT NURSES", WHERE SHE BECAME
ROMANTICALLY ATTACHED TO A DOCTOR DESPITE THEIR
ABUSIVE RELATIONSHIP.

HOW DO JAPANESE POP CULTURE, ESPECIALLY ANIME AND MANGA, INFLUENCE YOUR WORK? WHAT IMPACT HAVE THEY MADE ON TAIWAN?

JAPANESE CULTURE HAD HAD IMMENSE INFLUENCE ON TAI-WAN SINCE IT CAME UNDER JAPANESE CONTROL (1895-1945). MY GRANDFATHER WAS EVEN EDUCATED IN JAPA-NESE. JAPANESE CULTURE HAS BEEN GRADUALLY INTER-NALISED BY TAIWAN AND ENGENDERED NORMS AND VALUES UNIQUE TO THIS PLACE, AS YOU CAN FIND BILLBOARDS FILLED WITH EROTIC POSTERS DISPLAYING JAPANESE PORN ACTRESSES AT TAIWANESE BETEL NUT STANDS, AND MANGA FIGURES AS GAME PRIZES AT LOCAL NIGHT MARKETS. EVEN THAT TAIWAN IS NO LONGER GOVERNED BY JAPAN, TAIWANESE ARE STILL VERY ATTACHED TO JAPANESE AND ADMIRE THEIR CULTURE. IN FACT, AFTER SEVERAL VISITS TO JAPAN, I REALISE THAT JAPANESE AND TAIWANESE SEE THE COUNTRY IN DISSIMILAR WAYS. TAIWANESE MAY HAVE VIEWED JAPAN AS A GLORIOUS COUNTRY AND MISSED OUT THE PROBLEMS. PERHAPS MY WORK IS A VISUALISATION OF JAPAN IN TAIWANESE'S MIND.

CAN YOU TELL US SOMETHING ABOUT 'SCREEN GENERATION'? WHO ARE THEY? DO YOU CONSIDER YOURSELF ONE OF THEM?

ON MRT (TAIWAN'S SUBWAY), VERY OFTEN THE COMMUTERS WOULD ONLY BEND THEIR HEADS, SLIDING A FINGER OVER THEIR PHONE DISPLAYS TO WHILE AWAY TIME. WE REFER TO THEM AS 'HEAD-DOWN GENERATION'. WITH SMARTPHONES, HOMEBODIES WHO COULD HAVE JUST SPENT A DAY STAR-ING AT SCREENS AT HOME ARE ALLOWED TO REPEAT THIS ACTION ANYTIME, ANYWHERE. PROBABLY BECAUSE I'M TOO USED TO READING ON LARGE SCREENS, I WOULD ALSO TAKE MY MACBOOK ALONG AS MY DELUXE FACE-BOOK CHECK-IN TOOL. OUR LIFESTYLE HAS TURNED ALMOST EVERYONE INTO A MEMBER OF THE 'SCREEN GENERATION'. WHAT'S WORTH NOTING IS THAT, WHILE MY GENERATION HAS AT LEAST EXPERIENCED A CHILDHOOD DURING WHICH WE TYPED AND WROTE LETTERS BY HAND, THE YOUNG

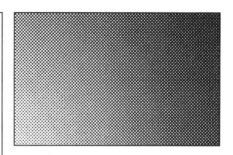

GENERATION HAVE ONLY GROWN UP PINCHING SMARTPHONE OR TABLET SCREENS. IT DESERVES ATTENTION AS TO WHAT KIND OF CHANGES THIS PHENOMENON COULD BRING TO THE FUTURE.

WHY IS FEMALE A RECURRING SUBJECT IN YOUR WORK? HOW ARE THEY DEPICTED IN THE CURRENT ANIME UNIVERSE?

I THINK FEMALE FIGURES ARE AES-THETICALLY PLEASING. AS A SHY 'HOMEBODY', I HAVE LOW SELF-ESTEEM AND ADORE FEMALES. THE WORLD OF MANGA HAS BEEN PORTRAYING FEMALES IN A CERTAIN MANNER. THE MORE USUAL TYPES ARE THE HELPLESS TIMID GIRLS-NEXT-DOOR AWAITING FOR THE MAIN CHARACTER'S RESCUE, AND THE PROUD, ARROGANT GIRLS WHO ALWAYS ACT AT WHIM, OR TAKE AD-VANTAGE OF THE MAIN CHARACTER

ALTHOUGH AGAINST HER HEART. THESE DEPICTIONS REALISE OTAKU'S IMAGINATION, DESPITE THE FACT THAT THEY MIGHT NOT EXIST IN THE REAL WORLD.

HOW DO YOU DRAW THE LINE BETWEEN EROTICA AND PORN?

FOR ME, BOTH 'EROTICA' OR 'PORN' ARE A PART OF LIFE. IN THIS 'SCREEN GENERATION' PERHAPS WE COULD ONLY GIVE AWAY THE TRUEST AND MOST NATURAL SELF IN FRONT OF A SCREEN. IT IS MY PRIME CONCERN ABOUT WHETHER MY WORK CAN COMMUNICATE THE THEME THAN WHETHER IT IS OBSCENE. EROTIC ART ARE POWERFUL AND EVOCATIVE. HOW THE PRODUCER MANAGES THE ENERGY WITHIN THE ELEMENTS WILL DEFINE THE RESULT.

JAPANESE PHOTOGRAPHY CRITIC KOTARO IIZAWA DESCRIBES YOUR "FLAT FLOWER" SERIES AS A TRUE EMBODIMENT OF JAPANESE OTAKU-CULTURE. WHAT IS OTAKU TO YOU?

IN JAPAN, THE TERM 'OTAKU' ORIGINALLY REFERS TO INDIVIDUALS WHO GRADUALLY DEVIATE THEMSELVES FROM THE MASS SOCIAL CULTURE FOR THEIR OBSESSIVE INVESTIGATIONS IN SPECIFIC SUBJECTS, FOR EXAMPLE, A 'TRAIN OTAKU (RAIL FANS)' CAN DETAIL ALL TRAIN MODELS AND STATION NAMES OF THE NATIONAL RAILWAY, WHILE I MAY BE MORE OF A 'CAMERA OTAKU' WHO TAKES PLEASURE IN COMPARING PHOTOGRAPHIC EQUIPMENTS. AND FOR 'ANIME OTAKU' WHO LACKS SOCIABILITY MAY JUST PROJECT THEIR FEELING OF AFFECTION TO ANIME CHARACTERS.

SUBSEQUENTLY, ANIMATION STUDIOS WOULD ADJUST THEIR CHARACTER DESIGNS ACCORDING TO WHAT THESE 'HOMEBODIES' DESIRE. THESE FICTIONAL AND EXCEPTIONAL CHARACTERS MAY BE UNREAL TO OTHERS, BUT HOMEBODIES' EYES THEY REPRESENT THE IDEAL LOVER WHOM THEY COULD INVEST PASSION AND LOVE IN.

HOW DIFFERENT IN YOUR OPINION IS TODAY'S PORTRAYAL OF POP CULTURE THAN IT WAS 20 YEARS AGO?

LOOKING BACK ON THE 90S, HARD-BOILED MANGA AND ANIME PREVAILED THE SCENE. LIKE, "AKIRA" BY KATSUHIRO OTOMO AND "KOKAKU KIDOTAI (GHOST IN THE SHELL)" BY MASAMUNE SHIROW, THESE WORKS CONTAIN CYPERPUNK SETTINGS AND REALISTIC DEPICTIONS. ON THE CONTRARY, 'MOE', THE MORE POPULAR GENRE TODAY, OFTEN CONTAINS VULNERABLE MALE CHARACTERS, AS WELL AS FEMALE CHARACTERS WITH RELATIVELY STRONG PERSONALITIES, WHO WOULD FREQUENTLY COMPEL MALE CHARACTERS TO TAKE UP A CERTAIN KIND OF CHALLENGES AND FORCE THEM TO MATURE. THIS IS ALSO RELEVANT TO THE PERCEPTIBLE CHANGES IN THE SOCIETY, WHERE MEN (USED TO BE TAUGHT TO BE BRAVE AND TOUGH) ARE SLOWLY TURNING INTO TIMID, PASSIVE 'HERBIVORE MEN' WHO TYPICALLY SHUN MARRIAGES AND LOVE RELATIONSHIPS.

WHAT IS THE MOST CHALLENGING ASPECT OF YOUR APPROACH? HOW DID YOU GET IT SORTED OUT?

WHEN I STARTED TO CREATE, IN A GENERATION WHERE IPAD WAS YET TO BE INTRODUCED, I HAD TO TACKLE PROBLEMS OF IMMOBILITY BROUGHT BY BULKY COMPUTER SCREENS, LIMITED SOCKET AND POWER SUPPLY. LATER WHEN IPAD FINALLY CAME, SCREENS BECOME MORE PORTABLE AS I CAN AFFIX THEM TO PHOTOGRAPHIC LAMP PODS.

WHAT IS YOUR FAVOURITE GRAPHIC NOVEL OR ANIMATED CARTOON? WHY IS IT SPECIAL TO YOU?

I GREW UP READING CLASSICS LIKE "DR SLUMP", "DRAGON BALL",

"YUYU HAKUSHO (GHOST FILES)," "BLACK JACK", ETC. I HAVE ALSO READ HONG KONG COMICS FOR SOME TIME, LIKE "FUNG WAN (WIND AND CLOUD)", WATCHED ANIME LIKE "KOKAKU KIDOTAI", "NEON GENESIS EVANGELION", AND PLAYED VIDEO GAMES LIKE "FINAL FANTASY" AND "GANBARE GOEMON". IN FACT, I DON'T HAVE PREFERENCE FOR ONE OVER ANOTHER. THEY ALL PIECE UP TO BECOME MY MEMORY AND GROWTH. WHILE I READ MANGA AND COMICS, I ALSO START LEARNING TO WRITE, PRACTISE DRAWING, AND FROM THE GAMES, I GAINED KNOWLEDGE AND LEARNED ABOUT HISTORY BIT BY BIT.

WHAT ARE YOU PLANNING ON DOING NEXT? IS THERE SOMETHING YOU'RE EAGER TO EXPLORE?

FOR NOW I WILL EXPAND "FLAWLESS LOVE", REALISING MY COLLECTION IN MORE REAL-LIFE SETTINGS AND SEE WHAT KIND OF WONDERS THESE SETTINGS COULD BRING TO MY WORK. SO, THERE WON'T BE JUST CARTOON FACES BUT MORE POSSIBILITIES, PROBING INTO THE PRESENT SOCIETY OR HISTORICAL ISSUES AROUND TAIWAN. BUT THAT WOULD REQUIRE MORE STUDIES AND RELEVANT LITERATURE TO FUEL MY CREATIONS WITH A RICHER AND MORE INTERESTING CONTEXT.

DIALOGUE WITH...
TEODORU BADIU!

WHAT DO YOU LOVE ABOUT POP ART AND CARTOONS? WHY DO YOU THINK IT IS EFFECTIVE TO GET YOUR IDEAS ACROSS THROUGH THIS MEDIUM?

I GREW UP WATCHING THE CLASSIC CARTOONS, FROM 20S TO 50S LIKE DISNEY, MAX FLEISCHER, TERRYTOONS OR UB IWERKS AND I LOVE THE LOOK AND FEEL OF THOSE CARTOONS SINCE THEN. POP ART STILL PLAYS A BIG ROLE ON THE ART MOVEMENT WORLDWIDE AND FOR ME IT FELT JUST RIGHT JUST TO PROJECT THE CLASSIC CARTOON CHARACTERS INTO THAT ART MOVEMENT FOR THE SIMPLE FACT THAT THEY SEEM TO FIT EACH OTHER PERFECTLY.

IS COMPLICATED IT COULD TAKE A FEW DAYS MORE. MOST OF THE TIME I COULD ONLY SPARE 1-2 HOURS AFTER OFFICE WORK TO DEVELOP MY CHARACTERS AND THEREFORE IT CAN TAKE A WEEK OR LONGER UNTIL A CHARACTER IS MADE.

WHY WOULD YOU REWORK SUPERHEROS AND FAIRYTALE CHARACTERS WITH SKULL FACES? ARE THEY STILL THE SAME SUPERHEROS AND CHARACTERS THAT WE KNOW?

FOR ME IT IS MUCH MORE INTERESTING TO CREATE WORLDS AND CHARACTERS THAT DON'T NECESSARY EXIST. I LOVE TO SEE HOW SOMETHING THAT I IMAGINE AND EXIST ONLY IN MY MIND COMES TO LIFE AND SUDDENLY EXIST THROUGH MY WORK. IT IS SIMPLY A LOT OF FUN TO GET RID OF ALL THE RATIONAL CONVECTIONS AND TO DECIDE MYSELF WHAT CAN BE REAL OR NOT. IT MAY BE SURREAL FOR SOME AND THE OTHERS WILL SIMPLY SAY THEY DO NOT EXIST BUT FOR ME IT BECOMES REAL THE MOMENT I CREATE IT. WHETHER THEY ARE STILL THE SAME CHARACTERS IS NOT IMPORTANT FOR ME. I JUST LET THEM LIVE THEIR OWN LIFE AND ALLOW THE AUDIENCE THE FREEDOM TO MAKE THE ASSOCIATIONS FOR THEMSELVES.

DO YOU CREATE 3D CHARACTERS FROM THE START OF YOUR CAREER? WHAT PROMPT YOU TO RENDER ILLUSTRATIONS INTO VOLUME?

AT THE BEGINNING OF 2000 I MOSTLY CREATED SURREAL PHOTO MANIPULATION USING PHOTOSHOP ON PHOTOS THAT I SHOT WITH MY DIGITAL CAMERA. FROM TIME TO TIME I ALSO SCAN DRAWINGS AND CREATE COLLAGES WITH PHOTOSHOP. ALL THOSE WORK IS STILL ONLINE AVAILABLE ON MY APOCRYH.NET WEBSITE.

ONE OF THE MAIN TRIGGERS WAS THE REBOOT TV SERIES AND PIXAR MOVIES BACK IN THE 90S. I LOVED THE CHARACTERS AND THE LOOK AND FEEL OF THE 3D WORLDS IN THOSE MOVIES AND I WANTED TO DO SOMETHING IN THAT DIRECTION. IT TOOK ME A FEW YEARS UNTIL I FOUND MY WAY INTO 3D, AND IN 2005, WHEN THE TIME WAS RIGHT, I SET UP THEODORU.COM TO CREATE 3D CHARACTERS AND ILLUSTRATIONS. I HAVE USED CINEMA 4D AT THE BEGINNING AND THEN FOR ABOUT 3 YEARS I HAVE SWITCHED TO THE FOUNDRY MODO WHICH I STILL USE TODAY.

WHAT KIND OF CREATURES DO YOU CREATE? DO THEY ALL HAVE PERSONALITIES? CAN YOU TELL US SOMETHING ABOUT YOUR CREATIVE PROCESS?

THEY COULD BE SMALL MONSTERS, SKULL BASED CHARACTERS, POP ARTTOONS, SEA CREATURES, KIDS, ETC. EVERYTHING THAT I CAN IMAGINE OR DREAM OF CAN BE CREATED. NOT ALL MY CHARACTERS HAVE PERSONALITIES BUT MOST OF THEM HAVE. I LIKE TO THINK THAT MY CHARACTERS ARE LIVING IN THEIR OWN WORLDS AND I ALSO LIKE TO CREATE INTERACTIONS BETWEEN THEM.

FOR ME THE CREATIVE PROCESS ENDS WITH THE DRAWING OF THE CHARACTER IDEA. WHAT COMES NEXT IS JUST WORK BASED ON THAT IDEA. IF I WORK ONLY ON ONE CARTOON CHARACTER I WILL NEED ABOUT 2-3 DAYS FOR MODELLING, TEXTURING AND RENDERING. IF THE CHARACTER

WHAT IS IT ABOUT WOOD TEXTURE AND GRAINS? WHAT DOES IT ADD TO YOUR WORK?

THE WOOD GRAIN HELPS GET RID OF THE COLOUR ASSO-CIATION AND TRANSPORT THE IDEA THAT I HAVE DESCRIBED BEFORE. TO CREATE CHARACTERS THAT DO NOT ACTUALLY EXIST IN THE REAL WORLD AND TO TRANSPORT THEM INTO THE CONTEXT THAT IS REAL AND TANGIBLE AND SO IT PUTS VIEWERS IN FRONT OF A DILEMMA ON HOW TO INTERPRET THESE ELEMENTS.

WHAT IS THE MOST CHALLENGING ASPECT OF YOUR APPROACH? HOW DID YOU GET IT SORTED OUT?

WHAT I TRY TO DO IS TO GIVE MY CHARACTERS THE LOOK AND FEEL OF THE CHARACTERS I LOVE AND THAT'S A SOURCE OF INSPIRATION FOR ME. THOSE ARE THE CHAR-ACTERS FROM THE CLASSIC CARTOON ERA SPANNING FROM THE 20S TO THE 50S. THAT INCLUDES AS WELL THE CLAS-SIC DISNEY CARTOONS AND OTHER WORKS OF UB IWERKS MADE FOR COMICOLOR CARTOONS AS WELL AS THE DAVE AND MAX FLEISHER CARTOONS OR THE TERRYTOONS, JUST TO NAME A FEW. I STILL WORK TO DEVELOP THAT PARTICU-LAR LOOK BUT I BELIEVE THAT I AM VERY CLOSE TO WHAT I WANT TO ACHIEVE WITH THE WORK THAT I CREATED FOR MY POP ARTOON PROJECT.

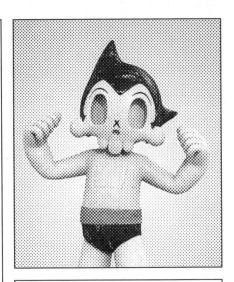

DO YOU COLLECT TOYS? WHAT ARE YOUR MAIN REFERENCE SOURCES?

YES I DO. I HAVE A BIG COLLEC-TION OF VINTAGE RUBBER TOYS AND IT'S STILL GROWING EVERY TIME I MAKE A VISIT TO THE FLEA MARKETS IN VIENNA AND THE CITIES THAT I VISIT. A BIG SOURCE OF INFLU-ENCE ON MY WORK HAS BEEN THE CLASSIC CARTOONS, FROM DISNEY, MAX FLEISCHER OR UB IWERKS, TO GRIM NATWICK BUT ANYTHING ELSE COULD BE A TRIGGER FOR AN IDEA FOR A NEW CHARACTER. IT COULD BE MUSIC, A MOVIE, BOOKS, GAMES, MAGAZINES, ETC.

WHAT IS YOUR FAVOURITE GRAPHIC NOVEL OR ANIMATED CARTOON? WHY IS IT SPECIAL TO YOU?

MY FAVOURITE COMICS ARE THE MICKEY MOUSE FROM THE 50S AND 60S AND MY FAVOURITE CARTOON CHARACTER FROM A MOVIE IS PI-NOCCHIO. I CAN'T EXPLAIN WHY. I SIMPLY LOVE THEM. IT COULD BE THAT BECAUSE THOSE CHARACTERS WERE THE FIRST ONES THAT I SAW AS A CHILD. I CAN STILL REMEMBER THAT I USED TO LOVE GOING TO THE THEATRES EACH SUNDAY MORN-ING JUST TO WATCH CARTOONS AND I DID THAT WITH GREAT PLEASURE.

HOW DIFFERENT IN YOUR OPINION IS TODAY'S PORTRAYAL OF POP CULTURE THAN IT WAS 20 YEARS AGO?

I THINK THAT POP CULTURE TODAY IS VERY RICH IN CONTENT AND ALSO VARIATION. IT IS PRESENT EVERY-WHERE AND ALL THE TIME. IT IS PART OF EVERY DAY LIFE AND IT IS WIDELY ACCEPTED BY PEOPLE.

WHAT ARE YOU PLANNING ON DOING NEXT? IS THERE SOMETHING YOU'RE EAGER TO EXPLORE?

I PLAN GET SOME MORE DIVERSIFI-CATION INTO MY PORTFOLIO, TO DO SOME MORE CUTE STUFF BESIDE MY POP ARTOONS WORK AND ALSO TO TRY TO SPEND MORE TIME CREATING MORE EDITORIAL AND ILLUSTRATION STYLE OF MY 3D WORK.

COMMONROOOM

30METHING SCARY (2011)

P.170-171

Stand-up comedy poster, premium and DVD packaging for Jan Lamb. Art directed by Jan Lamb. Poster photography by Sam Wong. Commissioned by East Asia Music (Holdings) Ltd.

GRASSHOPPER VS SOFTHARD (2012)

P.172

Concert poster and premium art-directed by Cantopop trio Grasshopper and rap duo Softhard. Poster photography by Sam Wong. Commissioned by Media Asia Entertainment Ltd.

BIG MAN (2012)

P.173

Poster for Edmond Leung's concert, BIG MAN. Photo by Wing Shya. Commissioned by Gold Typhoon Entertainment Limited.

30METHING ABOUT JAN LAMB — WOOOH (2010)

P.174-175

Packaging for Jan Lamb's album, A WOOOH. Art directed by Jan Lamb. Photo by Kiu@Shyalala. Commissioned by Gold Typhoon Entertainment Limited.

30METHING SCARY EP (2011)

P.176-177

Packaging for Jan Lamb's album, 30METHING SCARY. Art directed by Jan Lamb. Commissioned by East Asia Music (Holdings) Ltd.

D*FACE

SELECTED WORKS (2011-13)

P.228-239

Works showcased at D*Face's solo exhibitions "Going Nowhere Fast" at Corey Helford Gallery, Los Angeles, 2013 (P.234-235), "New World Disorder" at StolenSpace Gallery, London, 2013 (P.236-241) and numerous locations (P.242-245).

P.228 KISS OF DEATH (2011)

P.229 LEFT FOR DEAD (2011)

P.230-231 PRINT ROOM (2013)

P.232 ETERNAL REFLECTIONS (TOP, 2013), NO JOKE (BOTTOM, 2013)

P.233 BIG BOOM (TOP, 2013), FUUCK (BOTTOM, 2013)

P.234-235 WHAT'S UP CHARLIE BROWN (2013)

P.236 SNOOPY... DOWN & OUT (MELBOURNE, AUSTRALIA, 2011)

P.237 GUILTY PLEASURES (SHOREDITCH, LONDON, 2013)

P.238 HANDLE WITH CARE (TOP: WILLIAMSBURG, NYC, USA, 2012), LOVE HER, HATE HIM (BOTTOM: MANHATTAN, NEW YORK CITY, USA, 2012)

P.239 DON'T LOOK BACK (TOP: TOKYO, JAPAN, 2013), I'LL END THOSE DOGS (BOTTOM: MALAGA, SPAIN, 2013)

FANTASISTA UTAMARO

MANGACAMO & ONOMATOPOEIC CAMO

P.138

Textile design as inkjet prints on fabric. ©fantasista utamaro/KOTOBUKISUN.

WHAT'S A FANTASISTA UTAMA-RO!? BY QUOTATION (2013)

P.139-141

mangacamo on Masami Nagasawa for magazine QUOTATION. Costume design by MIKIO SAKABE. Photo by Yoshiharu Ota. Commissioned by Matoi Publishing.

CYZO (2011)

P.143-145

Art direction and design for magazine CYZO. Photo by Mitsuaki Koshizuka. Modelling by Seira Kagami.

LA JAPONAISE (2012)

P.146-147

Illustrations for studio album "La Japonaise" by Meg.

KAMINIETOMOJI (2012)

P.148-149

Art direction and book design for Japanese playwright and actress Motoya Yukiko's book.

MASTERMIND JAPAN (2012)

P.150

Artwork for a magazine published by menswear brand Mastermind Japan.

LUMINE X K-ON! (2011)

P.151

Design and art direction for a campaign launched by shopping mall Lumine Est.

TOKYO BAR NYC (2007)

P.152-155

Art direction and environmental design for a night pub in New York, in hands with mashmomix.

WE ARE TOKYO KARANKORON (2013)

P.156-159

Design and art direction for album "We are Tokyo Karankoron" by Japanese pop band Tokyo Karankoron. Photo by Patrick Tsai.

FORMA & CO

RE-VISION — POP CULTURE ICONS (2012)

P.182-187

Studio work as an exercise in style and synthesis of different cultural icons from comics, films, sports, television and music. Photo by Roc Canals.

JEFF HONG

UNHAPPILY EVER AFTER (2014)

P.094-099

Digital art showing a stark contrast between the happy pristine Disney fairytale characters in the world we live in.

JON WALTERS CREATIVE

HALLOWEEN INVITATION (2013)

P.240-241

A postcard invitation for Walter's annual Halloween party inspired by the works of EC Comics and Roy Lichtenstein. Photo by CSA Images / French Paper.

JONATHAN CALUGI

SUPER HERO (2013)

P.188-195

Limited art prints and illustrations for a zine imagining fatty heroes.

JUMPFROMPAPER

I GIVE MYSELF PERMISSION TO BE ME (2013-14)

P.074-079

A colourful line of bags, wallets and backpack playing on visual characters of cartoons and comics to fulfil user's childhood fantasy in real life.

LAZY OAF

LAZY OAF X LOONEY TUNES (2013)

P.202-207

A special collection celebrating people's love for the classic Looney Tunes cartoon iconography by highlighting the maniacal personalities of selected popular characters. Photo by Sam Hiscox. Set design by Anna Lomax. Hair and makeup by Teresa Davies. Modelling by Sarah Dick and Felix Radford. Licensed by Warner Brothers.

LAZY OAF X GARFIELD (2014)

P.208-213

A special collection celebrating Jim Davis' proud creation in a lightheartedly bold palette for Spring/Summer 2014. Photo by Michael Mills. Set design by Rosie Nicholas. Licensed by Bulldog.

MANASSEH LANGTIMM ASSOCIATES

BLACK HAND CELLARS (2010)

P.260-261

Self-initiated branding for the official wine of La Mano Nera (The Black Hand), a 20th century Italian extortion racket. Designs were made based on old pulp film noir posters, depicting suspected scenes of great danger just beyond the labels' periphery.

MAREK OKON

SPEED WINS (2013)

P.086-089

Out-of-home and print advertisements for NIKE Japan, in support of the NIKE-sponsored universities for a relay running race in Japan. oncept and production by Wieden+Kennedy Tokyo. Art by Sige.

MARK DREW

DEEZ NUTS (2013)

P.116-119

Artwork combining classic rap lyrics with Peanuts cartoons to pay homage to two of the Australian artist's obsession for his solo show at China Heights Gallery, Sydney, Australia, 2013.

P.116 JOINT (TOP), AGAIN (BOTTOM)

P.117 MY POSSE (TOP), DOGGHOUSE (BOTTOM)

MARKUS HOFKO

CARTOON PARTICLES (2008)

P.090-093

3D rendering analysing the components of renowned cartoon characters. Examined characters include Mickey Mouse, Donald Duck, Goofy and one of the Beagle Boys from Walt Disney's comics and stories.

MARTÍN VITALITI

№47 (2012)

P.009-011

Collage realised with eight original frames from Secret Origins #4 (1986) by Roy Thomas and Mark Waid, featuring The Flash.

№13 (2011)

P.012

Collage made using a page from Corto Maltese (2003) authored by Hugo Pratt.

№08 (2011)

P.013

The Flash spanning time and space in a collage realised with eight identical, original frames from Secret Origins #4 (1986) by Roy Thomas and Mark Waid.

№20 (2011)

P.014-016

Collage realised with two original frames from SUPERMAN #24 (2005)authored by Gregory Rucka, Paul Pelletier and Rick Magyar.

№43 (2012)

P.018 (TOP)

Collage realised with an original frame from Daredevil Purgatorio #5 (1996) by J. M. DeMatteis.

№58 (2012)

P.018 (BOTTOM)

Collage realised with four original frames from Superman for All Seasons (2001) by Jeph Loeb and Tim Sale.

№44 (2012)

P.019

Collage realised with one original frame from CONSTANTINE (2005) by S. Seagle, R. Randall and J. Palmiotti.

№15 (2011)

P.020

A sequence of five panels corresponding to different pages diachronically and runing through the punched out book from start to finish.

№93 (2013)
P.021

Artwork made using multiple copies of the same punched out page, arranged in a helix shape, to create a series of tunnels/black holes in which the astronaut pops out from his panel.

№17 (2011)
P.022-023

A labyrinthine network of punched out pages where original characters were left to look lost in the frames.

MIKA TSUTAI

MANGA PLATES (2011)
P.044-049

Dishware incorporating manga frames and graphical narrative elements, allowing meals to be arranged like a page torn off from a manga book.

MOIO ASSOCIATES

MORTIMER MOUSE (2013)
P.224-227

Tee prints combining two iconic pop cultural and religious symbols as a special collaboration between Studio Moio and Brazilian street wear label, Storvo.

NOIR JEWELRY

NOIR JEWELRY X DC COMICS (2014)
P.286-293

A special jewellery collection designed to empower wearers through superheros like Catwoman, Wonder Woman, Batman and Superman, to coincide DC Comic's 75th anniversary.

NOTO FUSAI

MONOLOGUE STICKER (2009)
P.028-033

Speech bubble stickers made to personify homes and household appliances as if they speak.

P.028 MONOLOGUE WALL SOCKET 02 (TOP)

Stickers saying "What voltage would you like, for the next birthday present?" "100 volts!!"

P.028 MONOLOGUE WALL SOCKET 01 (BOTTOM)

Stickers saying "I heard, in foreign country, their shapes are like (shape) or even like (shape)!!" "Scary…"

P.029 MONOLOGUE DOORKNOB

Sticker saying "Did you wash your hand properly?"

P.030 MONOLOGUE WINDOW

Sticker saying "Once in a while, look at ME, not the outside."

P.031 MONOLOGUE MIRROR

Sticker saying "Don't stare at me.. I'm shy."

P.032 MONOLOGUE TOILET PAPER

Sticker saying "30cm maximum per person, please!"

P.033 MONOLOGUE CLOCK

Sticker saying "38, 39, 40, 41, 42… don't talk to me! I will miss the number!!"

ÓSCAR GUTIÉRREZ GONZALEZ

TRAVESTISMO CÓMICO (FUNNY TRAVESTY)
P.280-282, 284-285

Acrylic paintings portraying deconstructed superheroes symbolic of broken hopes and the lost of identities in modern culture.

DESHUMANIZACIÓN
P.283

Magazine cover speaking of the degradation of human dignity in the 21st century. Commissioned by Ethic magazine.

PAPERFORM

BERSERKERGANG (2012)
P.166-169

Pop-up invitation and mechanical pop-up runway for Romance Was Born's Berserkergang show at Sydney Fashion Week. Paperform also designed the high gloss paper gauntlets and cuffs worn by models at the show. Commissioned by Romance Was Born.

PHILIP COLBERT

RODNIK X PEANUTS (2013)
P.120-123

Special fall fashion collaboration between celebrated comics strip Peanuts and The Rodnik Band picturing Charlie Brown and rest of the gang as his friends hanging out in the Rodnik world. Photo by Andrew Farrar.

POP TILL YOU DROP (2013)
P.124-127

Conceptual object dresses taking pop art off the wall and incorporating it into a line of fun ready-to-wear fashion items. Photo by Andrew Farrar.

RÉMI NOËL

LONELY BATMAN (2004-12)
P.178-181

A monochrome photographic series capturing Batman as a solitary figure wandering in rural Texas. All works are exclusively produced with silver film in original states.

REX KOO

SIMPLE PEOPLE (2012-)

P.128-137

Personal illustration project based on grids and drawing inspiration from music, film and pop culture icons.

P.128 SIMPLE CHARLIE (2013)

P.129 SIMPLE SNOOPY (2013)

P.130-131 SIMPLE KYOJIN (EREN) (LEFT, 2013), SIMPLE ARMOR KYOJIN (CENTRE, 2014), SIMPLE 50 FEET KYOJIN (RIGHT, 2013)

P.132 SIMPLE BATMAN 1966 (2013)

P.133 SIMPLE BATMAN 2012 (2013)

P.134 SIMPLE SIMPSONS (2013)

P.135 SIMPLE DRAGONBALL (2013)

P.136-137 SIMPLE SAILORMOON (2013)

ROMANCE WAS BORN

BERSERKERGANG (2012)

P.160-165

A fashion collaboration with Marvel Comics, presented at Sydney's Mercedes-Benz Fashion Week in 2012. Elements were drawn from Marvel's artistry and printing, from their CMYK printing and colours, to the "Kirby dots" and heroic figures likes Doctor Strange, Hulk and Thor. Photo by Lucas Dawson.

SANDRA CHEVRIER

LA CAGE (2013)

P.264-279

An art series about women trying to break away from the society's twisted preconceptions which are literally asking them to become superheroes.

SCHEMATA ARCHITECTS

YCAM ARCHIVES EXHIBITION (2013)

P.050-055

Wood exhibition setting acknowledging Yamaguchi Center for Arts and Media's (YCAM) contributions and important role in bringing forward contemporary art and culture in Yamaguchi for the past ten years.

SHUN SASAKI

J-POP ICONS (2013)

P.068-073

A self-initiated poster collection portraying household Japanese manga and anime characters in simplified forms. Depicted characters include Crayon Shinchan, Chibi Maruko-chan, Anpanman and Kitaro.

SIM CHANG

FLAWLESS LOVE

P.056-067

A projection of Sim Chang's state of mind and perspective towards issues in life onto anime scenarios realised through photography. Screens are set up as a metaphorical devise to convey a notion that perhaps the virtual world is the reality to those addicted to it.

P.056 DAUGHTER DAY (2013)

A girl from senior high at Sawara, Chiba, amid Hinamatsuri (Doll's Day).

P.057 DRAGON QUEST (2013)

A girl before colossal statue in Tainan, Taiwan, symbolic of local's idolatry practices.

P.058 AKIBA STREET (2013)

A girl costumed in Lolita fashion at Akihabara, a Mecca of anime and nurturing ground of Otaku culture.

P.059 BETEL NUT BEAUTY (2013)

A girl selling betel nuts at brightly-lit Taiwan roadside kiosks.

P.060 I LOVE SWIMMING (2012)

A girl floating in a pool of forgotten memories and things waiting to be recycled.

P.061 COMIC BED (TOP, 2010)

The first piece of Flawless Love. Lovelorn Chang compared his story to a nurse's struggle in Japanese anime Night Shift Nurses.

P.061 COFFEE AND GLOBALISATION (BOTTOM, 2013)

A girl enjoying a good coffee and sharing a wonderful moment with Mr Alpaca, regardless of the excessive costs involved in brewing the coffee.

P.062-063 CAMERA LOVE (2014)

A depiction of how photography enthusiasts are tied by their desire for new camera equipment.

P.064-067 NICE TO MEET YOU, SWIMMING POOL, BOOK STORE (2014)

Scenes evocative of the awkwardness of young lovers' first date.

TEODORU BADIU

DEAD WOOD (2014)

P.214-215

Art prints created for both adults and children for a Pop Artoons Exhibition at Atelier Olschinsky Art Store, Vienna, May 2014. Special thanks to Atelier Olschinsky Art Store.

SKULLTOONS (2014)

P.216-223

Art prints inspired by Dead Wood and produced as a hybrid between selected classic cartoon characters and Teodoru's iconic skull design. SkullToons was also part of Pop Artoons Exhibition, Vienna, May 2014. Special thanks to Atelier Olschinsky Art Store.

THE CREATIVE METHOD

HOLY WATER (2011)

P.262-263

A set of six wine labels featuring horror-style comic strips, reminding party-goers of what the end of the year party would look like. Illustration by Jason Paulos of The Drawing Book.

THEROOM CREATIVE LTD.

ETE! FALL/WINTER (2013)

P.080-081

A fall and winter launch campaign for ete!, a footwear and accessories boutique in Hong Kong with four anime characters. Illustration by zach. Commissioned by i.t Apparels Ltd.

ETE! SPRING/SUMMER (2013)

P.082-085

A spring and summer launch campaign for ete! visually evoking
a young and dynamic feeling with
manga style illustrations. Illustration by zach. Commissioned
by i.t Apparels Ltd.

TOMASZ PŁONKA

MOUSE (2013)

P.242-243

Screenprint on paper presenting
the famous mouse in a child's
dark inner universe, just as
Neil Gaiman's Coraline discov-
ered Other Father from another
world.

DUCK TALES (2013)

P.244

Screenprint on paper illustrat-
ing misery, misfortune and bane.
A moment of transformation that
takes place just before the men-
tal image collapses and before
the end or beginning of something else.

PLUTO (2013)

P.245

Screenprint on paper imagining
senescence occuring to old pal
Pluto after the years.

ARTISTS' BIO

BADIU, TEODORU

P.214-223

Teodoru Badiu is an illustrator, character designer and 3D artist. Based in Vienna, Austria, Badiu works with different media, from vector and traditional drawing, to collage or mixed media. The way of combining all those elements helped him to develop a very unique graphic style with bright but slightly dark messages. His cheerful, bizarre and colourful characters might be menacing on the outside, but are friendly by nature.

BUTCHER BILLY

P.246-255

Based in Curitiba, Brazil, Bily Mariano da Luz (aka Butcher Billy) is a creative director at a digital creative agency by day and a visual artist at other time. Da Luz' influences include Steve Ditko, Banksy, Tarantino, Jack Kirby, Tony Wilson, Salvador Dali, Malcom McLaren, Andy Warhol, Stanley Kubrick, Hanksy, and D※Face.

CALUGI, JONATHAN

P.188-195

Each of Jonathan Calugi's work is a take on his quirky childlike doodles with clean minimal lines and simple colours. Some of his recent projects include artist limited series for delonghi, uniqlo and fubon art gallery. The Italy-based illustrator was nominated for Print Magazine's New Visual Artists.

CHANG, SIM

P.056-067

Sim Chang's work has been recognised by Advertising category of PX3 (Paris) and Higashikawa International Photo Festival's Red Warehouse Selection Excellence Award in 2012 (Japan). Chang's visual language communicates reality with imaginary possibility in current 'Screen Generation', showing the gap and contrast between ordinary life shell and its flesh and bone. Kotaro Iizawa, famous critique of photography art from Japan, describes Chang's "Flat Flower" series as "a true understander if Japanese Otaku-culture".

CHEVRIER, SANDRA

P.264-279

Working in a home studio, Chevrier aggressively pursues a common thread until it is worn away, leaving her to begin on a new path. Her work is shown in Canada as well as the States, the UK, Europe and Asia. The series "Super Heros Cages" obtains a worldwide success. Her art is collected across Europe, the States, the Netherlands, New Zealand, Russia and Japan.

CHRIS PANDA

P.034-043

Chris 'Panda' Mercier is a French freelance illustrator who works with magazines, advertising agencies and other platforms on product and graphic design. Besides his personal projects such as the "Xray"s, he also challenges himself to produce his own comic book in the future.

COLBERT, PHILIP

P.120-127

Philip Colbert's his brand The Rodnik Band is a pop band rather than a traditional fashion label. The collection combines music, art and fashion to create a unique fashion concept. Colbert has picked up important supporters along the way, such as Karl Lagerfeld, Anna Piaggi and Lady Gaga, and was described "the Godson of Andy Warhol" by journalist Andre Leon Talley.

COMMONROOOM

P.170-177

Hong Kong-based design studio COMMONROOOM's strength lies in producing bold and memorable graphic design and art direction, whatever the application. Their impressive client list contains Pepsi, Giordano, Universal Music, Cartier and Wing Shya.

D*FACE

P.228-239

D※Face is a leading British contemporary urban artist as well as founder and curator of StolenSpace Gallery in London. His work is defined as 'aPopcalyptic': a satirical look at consumerism and our obsession with fame, pop culture, and all things celebrity.

DREW, MARK

P.116-119

Mark Drew is an Australian graphic artist and co-founder of China Heights Gallery in Sydney. His artwork revolves around pop culture references and 90s rap samples. He has been based in Tokyo, Japan, since 2009.

FANTASISTA UTAMARO
P.138-159

Fantasista Utamaro belongs to the new generation of entrepreneurial young Japanese artists who defy boundaries with diverse activities. Eager to embrace any and all forms of visual expressions, Utamaro works as a manga artist, textile designer and animation director, bringing his ultra pop and technicolour sensibilities to all with an explosive and fun energy unmistakably his own.

FORMA & CO
P.182-187

Forma is an independent studio from Barcelona dedicated to graphic communications. Founded by Joel Lozano and Dani Navarro, it works on corporate identity, communication strategy, editorial design, illustration, animation and web projects. Forma believes in the essence of things, in concepts, in order, in the economy of resources, in austerity and in clear and direct messages.

FROST, BEN
P.100-115

Ben Frost's work places common iconic images from advertising, entertainment and politics into startling juxtapositions. Originally from Australia, he currently works out of his studio in Montreal, Canada. Most commonly known for his 'mash-up' style of hyper-saturated Pop Art that critiques our consumerist lifestyles, he is currently exploring painting onto packages and found objects.

GUTIÉRREZ GONZALEZ, ÓSCAR
P.280-285

Óscar Gutiérrez Gonzalez is a graphic artist and illustrator who works passion on advertising art. Influenced by Lowbrow, poster design, urban culture, comics and American pop culture, Gutiérrez Gonzalez currently explores techniques of collage and graphic compositions for high visual impact.

HOFKO, MARKUS
P.090-093

Markus Hofko has been working as an artist, designer and musician for most of his life. After his communication design studies and work in Augsburg, he moved to Auckland in 2007 where he works independently for art, cultural, music and advertising fields. He creates designs, videos and conceptual photos for Wired magazine, Adidas, Diesel, and many more.

HONG, JEFF
P.094-099

Jeff Hong is an animation artist based in New York City. His career started as a clean up artist at Walt Disney Feature Animation for films like Hercules, Mulan, Tarzan, and The Emperor's New Groove. He graduated from the Rhode Island School of Design with a BFA in Illustration in 2004 and continues working in animation as a storyboard artist.

JON WALTERS CREATIVE
P.240-241

A graphic designer based in Chicago, Jon Walters is interested in the uncommon beauty of common things, found art, thrift stores, Polaroids and handmade items.

JUMPFROMPAPER
P.074-079

Launched in 2010 by Taiwanese designers Chay Su and Rika Lin, JumpFromPaper is a line of playful bags created with cartoon-like colours and 2D styling. Armed with the philosophy of "Why take everything so serious?", the designer-duo combines 2D graphics and 3D illusion to create a truly distinct bags. Started as a small run, JumpFromPaper is now available in over 25 countries worldwide.

KOO, REX
P.128-137

Rex Koo is a Hong Kong-based graphic artist for more than a decade. His work features a breadth of local music albums and movie poster design. He has also been a participating artist in Nike Hong Kong, Homeless Dictator (Finland 2008), Get It Louder (China 2007) and The Place Project (Barcelona 2005). Recently, Koo blends graphic design and hand-drawn elements in the middle of his creative career, and devotes himself to painting as his main pursuit.

LAPRAY, BENOIT
P.294-303

Born in 1980 in Bourgogne (France), Benoit Lapray studied Art, Journalistic Communication and Photography at school (in Lyon, France). Having been a full time advertising photographer and retoucher for five years in Haute-Savoie, he moved to Lyon before settling down in Paris in 2014, working as freelance photo retoucher in commercial photography. Next to his own photographic work, he also writes about contemporary photography.

LAZY OAF
P.202-213

Lazy Oaf is a London-based label designing bright bold clothing and accessories for men and women. Founded by Gemma Shiel in 2001, the brand began life as a small screen printers in Spitalfields. Lazy Oaf collections are notoriously colourful, cartoon inspired and heavy on nineties nostalgia. Their design philosophy is not trend driven, but focusing on a unique directional vision referencing street wear and all things weird and eccentric. Exclusive collaborations include Batman, Kickers, Nasty Gal and Looney Tunes.

MALIK, ASLAN
P.256-259

Creative director Aslan Malik graduated from the Berliner Technical Art School in 2005 with a BFA in Multimedia Design. He works in his hometown Berlin after graduation and has been pursuing opportunities in Shanghai, Tokyo, Beijing and New York since 2010, creating forward-thinking work for clients such as Porsche, BMW, MINI, Absolute Vodka, Mercedes and Universal Music and on his way winning awards at the Cannes Lions festival and Red Dot the ADC Europe.

MANASSEH LANGTIMM ASSOCIATES
P.260-261

Portland-based Manasseh Langtimm Associates specialises in special graphics done with both computers and by hand as well as artistic guidance and creative direction. They also work hand in hand with Walter Warren Walters with the import and export of fine clothing for men and women.

MOIO ASSOCIATES
P.224-227

Developed by a group of designers, advertisers and fashion designers, Moio seeks to combine several specialties and platforms in forging creative projects, both analogue and digital. The mixture of different talents constitutes Moio dynamics, which, go beyond the core of professional partnerships to optimise and facilitate the execution of works.

MORBACH, ARMIN
P.196-201

For the past two decades, Armin Morbach has been an in-demand stylist and has worked with the best photographers, including Michel Comte, Patrick Demarchelier, Karl Lagerfeld, Ellen von Unwerth, and Peter Lindbergh. Driven by a desire to continue developing his artistic expression and to perfect his visions in presentation, he took the next logical step and picked up a camera. Morbach and his work are now part of the NRW Forum's State of the Art Photography exhibition and are represented at the En Compagnie de Guy Bourdin retrospective at the Deichtorhallen in Hamburg. He is also the publisher and editor-in-chief of TUSH magazine.

NOËL, RÉMI
P.178-181

Rémi Noël is not one of those people who started photography at six with their grandfather's Rolleiflex. He was already 30 when he felt compelled to create images and shot a few still lives in his Paris apartment. As a photographer, he tries to tell brief stories captured at a glance. He quickly left Parisian interiors behind to embark on annual ten-day expeditions to the American West, where he explores the archetypes of American mythology in black and white.

NOIR JEWELRY
P.286-293

Since its inception in 1994, nOir has established a deep brand following due to creative director Leeora Catalan's forward thinking and ability to push the limits of conventional jewellery design. By infusing many influences such as historical fashion icons and present day pop culture, the nOir brand encompasses urban modern glamour and wearable works of art.

NOTO FUSAI
P.028-033

Noto Fusai is a product designer duo and wedded couple, Noto Hirotsugu and Noto Miyo. With "Noto" being their last name, "Fu" and "Sai" mean husband and wife respectively. Believing that human has pushed civilisation forward little by little by improving their tools and perspectives toward them, their expectations for product-making lies on whether it is challenging the frontier of civilisation.

OKON, MAREK
P.086-089

For the last eight years Marek Okon has worked at Wieden+Kennedy Tokyo as designer, art director, photographer, illustrator, and animator interchangeably. He has collaborated with clients like Honda, Nike Japan, Google, MTV, Sony Playstation Japan, Sony VAIO, Ben & Jerry's Ice Cream, and W+K Tokyo Lab. His multidisciplinary approach to design comes from a passion to play the roles of craftsman and inventor to bring ideas visually and conceptually to life.

PAPERFORM
P.166-169

Benja Harney is a self-taught paper engineer based in Sydney, Australia. Paper is his passion and through his business, Paperform, Harney engineers high-end pop-up books and crisp paper constructions professionally spanning a variety of applications such as fine art, advertising, magazine illustration, fashion and packaging.

PŁONKA, TOMASZ
P.242-245

Tomasz Płonka is a graphic designer and illustrator based in Warsaw, Poland. Inspired by comics and cartoon animations, he develops an otherworldly body of work that all together constructed a darker universe.

ROMANCE WAS BORN
P.160-165

Anna Plunkett and Luke Sales met whilst studying fashion design and launched their Sydney-based label in 2005. The designers take inspiration from artists, often working with them collaboratively to create a unique language each season. The pair are known for their ambitious and often theatrical runway shows. Previous collaborations have been realised with artists like Del Kathryn Barton and Kate Rhode.

SASAKI, SHUN
P.068-073

Shun Sasaki is Tokyo-based graphic designer born in 1985.

SCHEMATA ARCHITECTS
P.050-055

Jo Nagasaka was born in Osaka. After graduating from the Department of Architecture, Tokyo University of the Arts, he established Schemata Architects in 1998. In 2007, he started a collaboration office called HAPPA, a combination of a gallery, shop and other facilities. His work includes Sayama Flat, 63.02, PACO, HOUSE OKUSAWA, Aesop Aoyama/Ginza, MR.DESIGN, LLOVE and HANARE, Today's Special Jiyugaoka/HIkarie and Hue plus. He released UDUKURI, a series of "Flat Table" from Established and Sons in 2012.

THE CREATIVE METHOD
P.262-263

The Creative Method was established in 2005 with a sole purpose of creating the best designs off the back of even better ideas. They focus on creating brands that have impact, standout, with a point of difference. They like to stay small and flexible. They believe that by understanding the principles of great design combined with clear and simple ideas they can work on any discipline.

THEROOM CREATIVE LTD.
P.080-085

THEROOM is a creative consultancy specialising in branding, multimedia art direction and graphic design - websites, mobile apps, interactive installations and much more. THEROOM aspires to be a humble interpreter to their audience and for their clients through creative design and commercial art, while simultaneously showing sophistication and perfection through their work.

TSUTAI, MIKA
P.044-049

Mika Tsutai is a product designer from Kyoto, Japan. Graduated from Kyoto Institute of Technology in Product Design in 2011, she worked as an in-house designer for two years and is now working freelance.

VAN HOEY, ANN
P.024-027

Ann Van Hoey was born in Mechelen, Belgium in 1956. She graduated from the University of Antwerp in 1979 with a Masters degree in Applied Economic Sciences. In 2008, she was rewarded the Henri Van de Velde-label for prestigious Belgium design and also a winner at Belgium's International Design Competition in 2010. She is a member of the International Academy of Ceramics.

VITALITI, MARTÍN
P.009-023

Martín Vitaliti (Buenos Aires, 1978) studied Fine Arts at the Manuel Belgrano National School in Buenos Aires. He has been living and working in Barcelona since 2002. In 2012 he was awarded the Museo ABC drawing prize and had a solo exhibition at the museum (Madrid, 2013); Generación 2013 Prize, Obra Social Caja Madrid (Madrid, 2013); Marco Magnani Prize-Young artists (Sardinia, 2013). Many of Vitaliti's works are the private and public collections of Fundación Caja (Madrid), Biblioteca Nacional de España, ICArt Collection (Miami), Colección Centre d'Art La Panera, Colección Mengs, among others.

426411

ACKNOWLEDGEMENTS

We would like to thank all the designers and companies
who have involved in the production of this book. This
project would not have been accomplished without their
significant contribution to the compilation of this book.
We would also like to express our gratitude to all the
producers for their invaluable opinions and assistance
throughout this entire project. The successful completion
also owes a great deal to many professionals in the
creative industry who have given us precious insights
and comments. And to the many others whose names are not
credited but have made specific input in this book, we
thank you for your continuous support the whole time.

FUTURE EDITIONS

If you wish to participate in viction:ary's future
projects and publications, please send your website or
portfolio to submit@victionary.com